CONGRATULATIONS

to the best team in CART* on another great season

© 2000 Target Stores

*Determined by a very proud and somewhat biased sponsor

TARGET

Red Byron became the first
NASCAR winner in 1948.

to a winner, there are no disadvantages, only other challenges on the way to victory.

It was 1948, almost half a century after Henry Ford's first and only auto race marked the beginning of Ford track history in 1901. On a beach-and-road course just south of Daytona, Marshall Teague, at the wheel of a '39 Ford, made history as the first driver to lead a lap in a NASCAR event. Fonty Flock, also in a '39 Ford, created the first lead change in the 35th lap. But Red Byron, *also* in a '39 Ford, became the first NASCAR-sanctioned winner with a 15-second victory over Teague. Not bad for a guy whose war injury required his left foot to be fixed to a stirrup attached to the clutch pedal. It's this kind of pride and desire for perfection that goes into the 2001 Taurus, and into every car and truck we build.

Log on to the legend of Ford Racing at
www.fordracing.com

1901 **100** 2001
Years

W E   R A C E .   Y O U   W I N™.

COMEBACK OF THE YEAR... Marlboro Team Penske
Roger Penske, the architect of more Champ Car victories (99) and championships (7) going into the 2000 season, reversed the course of two lackluster previous years by taking the FedEx Championship with new driver Gil de Ferran, above. De Ferran won twice and the team got an additional boost from their other new recruit Helio Castroneves who scored three times. A new Honda, Reynard, Firestone equipment package was the foundation of the team's success.

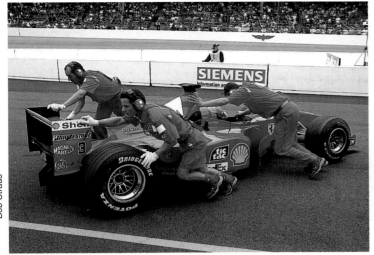

Michael Schumacher

Gil de Ferran

Brian Simo

Buddy Lazier

James Weaver

WINNING WHEELS

What do Formula One's Michael Schumacher, CART's Gil de Ferran, IRL's Buddy Lazier, Grand American's James Weaver and Trans-Am's Brian Simo have in common? All were the 2000 champions in their series and all rolled to their titles on BBS wheels. Add to that list Olivier Beretta who was the American Le Mans Series GT champion and the overall winner of the Rolex 24 at Daytona. NASCAR's Bobby Labonte didn't make the lineup of champion BBS users. That series mandates steel wheels, not the light alloy type that BBS makes.

COUP OF THE YEAR... Indianapolis 500 Falls to Target/Ganassi's Juan Montoya. Target/Chip Ganassi Racing, with four consecutive CART FedEx Championships in their logbooks, but no previous Indy Racing Northern Light Series experience invaded the rival series' premier event, the Indianapolis 500, and came away with the victory, courtesy of CART champion Juan Pablo Montoya. Teammate Jimmy Vasser finished seventh.

BBS. Seen in all the right circles.

It was a very good year for BBS.
We were in the F1 winners circle nine times in 2000.

Formula 1 Driver and Constructor World Champion,
CART FedEx Champion,
IRL Champion, SCCA Trans Am Champion,
ALMS-GTS & GT3 Champion,
Grand American Series – SRI, AGT, GTU,
and Motorola Cup – SGS Champion

Call for your nearest BBS dealer at 1 800 422-7972.

BBS. The Choice of Champions.

BBS
The Choice of Champions.
BBS of America • 5320 BBS Drive, Braselton, GA 30517

Winston Cup Winner BOBBY LABONTE captured Driver of the Year honors prior to his starring role at the NASCAR Awards dinner before a sellout black-tie crowd in the Grand Ballroom of New York's Waldorf-Astoria.

WIN THE NASCAR WINSTON CUP CHAMPIONSHIP AND YOU'LL DEVELOP QUITE A FOLLOWING.

Pontiac's WideTrack Attack Team congratulates drivers' champ Bobby Labonte.

Three words: Bobby's the man. He led the outnumbered Pontiac WideTrack™ Attack Team to its best year ever and in return got to take home the mantle-dwarfing NASCAR® Winston Cup trophy. And obviously Bobby isn't the only one who knows the secret of WideTrack Handling. Which leads us to another three words: Wider is Better.

The WideTrack Grand Prix.
Wider is Better.

An illustrious history for American manufacturers in Daytona's endurance classic

1965... Ford's all conquering MKI, driven by Ken Miles and Indy car driver Lloyd Ruby, crossed the finish line first, followed by three other Fords for a four car sweep of top honors.

1966... Ken Miles and Lloyd Ruby won again, this time in a Ford MKII. The next two cars to finish were also Fords, a three car sweep.

All photos: Daytona Racing Archives

1969... a pair of Lola Chevrolets, entered by Roger Penske, scored a 1-2 finish. The late Mark Donohue and Chuck Parsons piloted the winner.

1995... Paul Newman co-drove a Mustang to the GTS win, third overall. Michael Brockman, Tommy Kendall, and NASCAR star Mark Martin were the co-drivers.

10

1996... Oldsmobile powered the winners, Wayne Taylor, Indy car driver Scott Sharp and Jim Pace did the driving.

1997... Ford was back in the victory limelight in Rob Dyson's R&S MKIII. Elliot Forbes-Robinson, Butch Leitzinger, and John Paul Jr. were the drivers.

1999... A second victory for Rob Dyson's R&S Ford MKIII. Andy Wallace joined the Elliot Forbes-Robinson, Butch Leitzinger driving team.

2000... Grand Touring cars had come close before. But Dodge scored the ultimate endurance victory with its Viper, first overall in the Rolex 24 at Daytona classic, humbling all the lighter, faster prototypes. Olivier Beretta, Karl Wendlinger and Dominique Dupuy shared the driving duties.

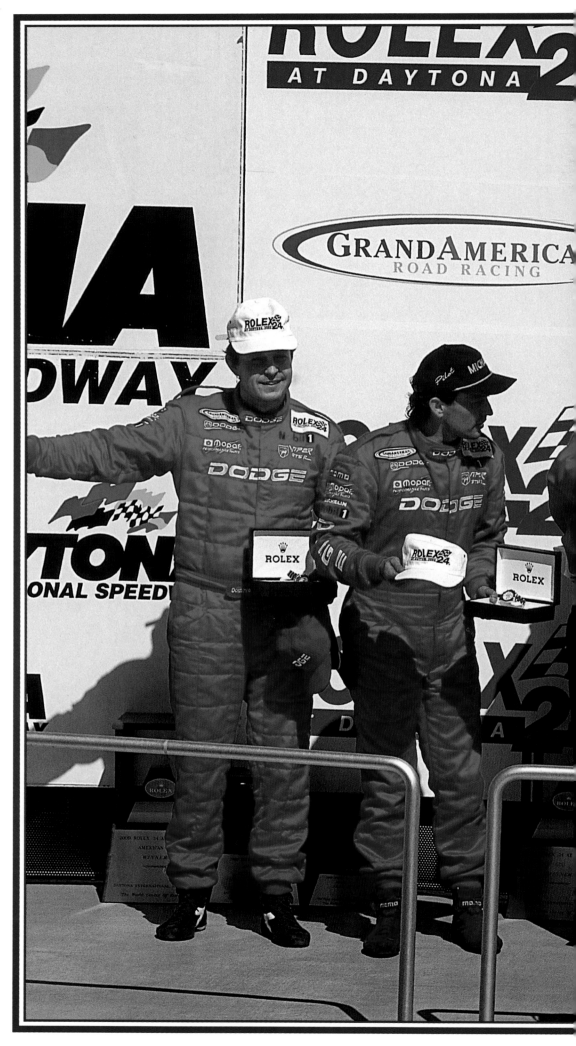

Walter Fischer, right,
Rolex Watch USA
President and CEO,
expanded the company's
watch awards in 2000.
Class winners, as well as
the overall victors,
Olivier Beretta,
Karl Wendlinger and
Dominique Dupuy, will
get handsome Rolex
timepieces.

13

For those who are extremely driven.
But also like to drive.

The Rolex Cosmograph is one of the most versatile timepieces in the Rolex collection. With three recorders that register elapsed hours, minutes and seconds, a large stopwatch sweep-second hand and a graduated bezel, it can precisely measure elapsed time and indicate average speed or rate of production. Naturally, the Cosmograph is the watch of choice for hard-driving individuals whether at the helm of a company or the wheel of a racecar.

ROLEX

CONTENTS

CART FedEx Championship

Dayton Indy Lights

Barber Dodge Pro Series

NASCAR Winston Cup

NASCAR Craftsman Truck Series

Indy Racing Northern Light Series

Grand American Road Racing Association

Professional Sports Car Racing American Le Mans Series

BFGoodrich Tires Trans-Am Series

Formula One World Championship

PUBLISHED BY: Autosport International, Inc.
PUBLISHER: John H. Norwood
ASSOCIATE PUBLISHER: Barbara Hassler-Steig
DESIGN DIRECTOR: Robert Steig
EDITOR: Jonathan Hughes
FRONT COVER PHOTOGRAPHY: Richard Dole, Ken Hawking, Nigel Kinrade, Steve Swope
CONTRIBUTING PHOTOGRAPHERS: Cheryl Day Anderson, Dan Bianchi, Brian Czobat, Richard Dole, Ronda Greer, Ken Hawking, Nigel Kinrade, Bob Steig, Bob Straus, Steve Swope, David Trimble
PHOTOGRAPHY CONTRIBUTED BY: Daytona Racing Archives, Indianapolis Motor Speedway, Texas Motor Speedway

MOTORSPORTS AMERICA, THE MEN & MACHINES OF AMERICAN MOTORSPORT, 2000-01
IS PUBLISHED BY AUTOSPORT INTERNATIONAL, INC.
37 EAST 28 STREET, SUITE 408, NEW YORK, NY 10016
© 2001 AUTOSPORT INTERNATIONAL, INC.
NO PART MAY BE REPRODUCED WITHOUT PRIOR WRITTEN PERMISSION.
DISTRIBUTED IN THE U.S. BY MOTORBOOKS INTERNATIONAL, OSCEOLA, WI 54020
PRINTED IN THE U.S.A.

FIREHAWK®—CART CHAMPIONS' TIRE 1996-2000

The lessons we learn on race day are in the tires you count on every day.

With a record 51 wins at the Indy 500® Firestone knows Indy racing like no other tire company. And if we can develop the kind of quick acceleration, grip and stability required for **CART** racing tires, just imagine how well our line of Firehawk street performance tires will perform for you. Firehawk performance tires are speed rated from S to Z and specially engineered for crisp handling and legendary performance. And now you have a choice of Firehawk street tires made with either **UNI-T**® or

UNI-T AQ™ technologies. **UNI-T**, the **U**ltimate **N**etwork of **I**ntelligent **T**ire **T**echnology, is designed to deliver outstanding wet performance, especially wet stopping, while still providing excellent dry performance. And **UNI-T AQ** Ultimate Tire Technology adds the power of **EPO**™ (**E**xtended **P**erformance **O**ptimization) with Dual-Layer Tread™. So even as its tread wears down, its wet performance stays up. For outstanding wet braking. See your local Firestone retailer and check out the complete line today.

Firehawk SZ50 EP
with UNI-T AQ
Z-Speed Rated Ultra-High
Performance Street Tire

Firehawk SH30
with UNI-T
H-Speed Rated High
Performance Street Tire

Firehawk SS20 with UNI-T
S & T-Speed Rated
Performance Street Tire

Firehawk
Indy® Racing Slick

BORN AT INDY.®
PERFORMS EVERYWHERE.™

1-800-807-9555
www.firestonetire.com

Indianapolis 500,® Indy 500® and Indy® are registered trademarks of the Indianapolis Motor Speedway.

Gil de Ferran Takes the Title for a Resurgent Marlboro Team Penske

New drivers, new equipment, new manager and, perhaps more importantly, a new attitude, were the hallmarks of the 2000 edition of Marlboro Team Penske. Recognizing the subpar performance of his "in house" Penske chassis, Ilmor engines, and long term star driver Al Unser Jr., "Captain" Roger Penske, the architect of more Champ Car victories and series titles than any other team owner, fired the lot. In their place at the end of the 1999 season came new drivers Gil de Ferran, an analytical veteran, and Helio Castroneves, a spirited young blood. They would be driving the proven Reynard-Honda-Firestone equipment package that won the last four championships. New team manager Tim Cindric was brought in to oversee the operation. Typical Penske thoroughness went into testing and refining the new equipment. So thorough was this process, that other Reynard users coined the term "Reynskes" for chassis deemed to have been massaged in Penske shops to a recognizable margin of superiority.

It didn't take long for the "new look" Marlboro Team Penske to serve notice that the lackluster days of recent history were over. In the season opener at Homestead, de Ferran claimed the pole and Castroneves was seventh fastest in qualifying. But for an unfortunately timed pit stop, de Ferran might have won and covered the new team with immediate glory. Instead, he was shuffled down to sixth place. Next time out at Long Beach, de Ferran again occupied the hotly contested pole position at the start, again had to postpone his first victory of the year. This time a nose section, crunched on a restart, was the culprit; a seventh place finish the result. Teammate Castroneves gave a hint of victories to come by registering a solid second place. The team's early season promise bogged down in the two overseas outings, Brazil and Japan, next on the schedule. De Ferran then hit pay dirt in the snow postponed Nazareth mile, owned, liked the team, by Maestro Penske. He scored the first victory for "new look" Marlboro Team Penske from fifth on the starting grid. Castroneves qualified on the second row but placed well outside the top 10. At Milwaukee, postponed by rain, neither Marlboro Team Penske driver posted sparkling results. On Detroit's tight, difficult street circuit, it was Castroneves' turn to bask in the winner's limelight. The newly constituted team got its second victory of the year and Penske was proved to be astute in his selection of de Ferran's teammate. At Portland, the Penske pair claimed both front row starting slots. Castroneves got the pole but de Ferran prevailed at the end. The pole winner was shuffled back to seventh at the finish. Although de Ferran counts Cleveland as one of his favorite CART tracks and he qualified on the front row, he finished midpack. Castroneves finished with the day's tailenders. Castroneves racked up another pole in Toronto but couldn't capitalize on it. De Ferran ended up just outside the top five. Chicago was podium territory for de Ferran but "no where" for Castroneves. At Mid-Ohio, Penske's well-honed chassis showed their mettle. De Ferran and Castroneves qualified one-two, finished one-two but in the reverse order. "Professor" de Ferran's student Castroneves was learning his lessons only too well. Elkhart Lake and Vancouver added little to the Penske pair's point total but at Laguna Seca they lit up the leader board. Castroneves, in his best outing to date, ran a picture perfect race, winning from the pole. De Ferran followed him across the line from the other front row starting position. At Gateway, the Marlboro Team Penske drivers picked up useful top 10 points. Houston afforded de Ferran the points for pole position and a third place finish. Castroneves also made the day's top five. Like the two previous overseas venues, Australia did little to upgrade the points totals for either. De Ferran could have nailed down the title here but a collision with Montoya ended that hope. Going into the season finale at Fontana, points leader de Ferran had a slim five point margin over an upwardly mobile Adrian Fernandez, who won in Australia. Paul Tracy, Kenny Bräck and Roberto Moreno also had theoretical, if unrealistic, shots at the title. A finely focused de Ferran claimed the Fontana pole, his fifth of the year. It was also a new world closed course record at 241.428 mph. Despite his speed advantage "Professor" de Ferran wasn't about to see his championship chances go up in the smoke of a blown engine. He played out his hand conservatively finishing third, comfort-

Dan Bianchi

1 Swift and smart, **GIL DE FERRAN** had just the right combination of talents to return a resurgent Marlboro Team Penske to the championship level. It was the team's eighth FedEx Championship Series title, de Ferran's first. (168 CART/FedEx Championship Series points)

ably ahead of fifth place Fernandez. His approach was totally justified. Fifteen of the 26 starters failed to finish, and de Ferran was the only Honda pilot to go the distance. "Professor" de Ferran had executed "Captain" Penske's game plan to perfection. The team owner possibly enjoyed this championship more than his earlier ones. Redemption is beautiful.

Adrian Fernandez should love the 2001 CART FedEx Championship schedule. New races in England and Germany have been added. The star Mexican driver thrives on overseas venues. He won two of the three 2000 events on tracks outside North America. While he didn't take the driver's championship, he was in the hunt right up to the Fontana finale, where he finished fifth to points leader and new champion Gil de Ferran, whose third place clinched the title. Short of the championship rung, Fernandez had his best season to date, runner-up in the title chase. He also achieved a long term goal with his announced debut as a team owner in 2001 with primary backing from long term sponsor Tecate and strong technical direction from ex-Ganassi chief Tom Anderson. He is a national hero in his native Mexico and well liked in the U.S. Both of his wins, Brazil and Australia, came from starts in the second half of the field. He completed 2601 laps, a higher total than any other driver. Both he and his teammate Roberto Moreno seemed to be able to extract better fuel mileage from their Ford engines than other pilots, a tribute to their Patrick Racing engineers and intelligent driving styles. Moreno, better known as a substitute driver who could quickly master strange machinery, just as quickly adapted as a regular in the Patrick group. He earned his first Champ Car victory in convincing fashion, from the pole, at Cleveland. He actually led the points parade briefly after his breakthrough triumph, and was theoretically in the final countdown for the championship at Fontana. He didn't win the season finale, but second place in the race gained him third place in the championship and made Patrick Racing the team with the highest finishing aver-

age of 2000. With Fernandez gone in 2001, he'll be the longest tenured pilot at Patrick. Along with new teammate Jimmy Vasser he'll be in a position to mount another challenge for the championship, this time with Toyota engines.

Officially a rookie, but hardly a beginner, Sweden's Kenny Bräck, the IRL transplant and the "new boy" on Bobby Rahal's team ran up front from the start. He led some laps in the season opener at Homestead, as he did in six other races. While a first CART victory did not materialize for the 1999 Indianapolis 500 winner and 1998 IRL champion, four podium appearances did. He earned runner-up honors at Cleveland and Australia and third place at Nazareth and Road America. Like Moreno, he had an outside chance at the championship going into the last event. Unlike Moreno, he didn't finish at Fontana. He did garner the point for the most laps led. With a full year's experience on the CART circuit, the runaway 2000 Rookie of the Year will be targeting higher honors in 2001.

The best two car team of 1999, Team KOOL Green, was nudged from that lofty perch in 2000. The off-season favorite for the 2000 title, Dario Franchitti, got off to an unfortunate start and never recovered. A "Spring Training" accident left him with a broken pelvis even before the season started. He recovered in time to start the opening Homestead event, but never recovered the form that saw him in victory circle three times in 1999 and tied in year end points with champion Juan Montoya. The closest he came were seconds in Japan and Vancouver. A pit lane miscue cost him the win in Vancouver and handed it to teammate Paul Tracy. Thirteenth in the championship, down from second the previous year, was the fate of this brilliant driver, a mid-season candidate for the Jaguar Formula One team. Instead of F1 he'll be back with Team KOOL Green in 2001, attempting to get back on track. By contrast, teammate Paul Tracy was very much on form. He was the early season points leader before running into an unwelcome series of DNFs. The Canadian ended the year with three victories, tied with Helio Castroneves

and Juan Montoya for the highest total of 2000. At Long Beach, he sliced his way through the field to victory lane from 17th starting position on a circuit where passing is notoriously difficult. His Road America win was even more spectacular. The Canadian came from dead last after an engine malfunction on the opening lap. His third win was a bit of a gift from teammate Dario Franchitti who stalled in the pits while in the lead. Like Bräck and Moreno, he had a long odds championship opening, prior to Fontana, but was never a factor there due to mechanical failure. While he slipped two places on the leader board to fifth, it was still a productive year for Tracy, who enters the 2001 season in the second year of his five year Team KOOL Green contract.

The 1996 FedEx Series champion, Jimmy Vasser, received notice from team owner Chip Ganassi well before 2000's season end that he wouldn't be invited back for 2001. Vasser got some balm for his wounds by winning the penultimate Houston race and landing a ride with Patrick Racing, the team with the year's best record. Winless in 1999, Vasser had to beat teammate Juan Montoya, generally acknowledged to be the circuit's fastest driver, to gain top honors in Houston. The win bounced him up to sixth in the year's points production. He'll be gunning for career victory number 10 when he goes to work for Patrick.

Roger Penske's bet on young Brazilian Helio Castroneves as the second driver on his revamped 2000 team paid off handsomely. Not only did Castroneves win, he scored three victories, tying for top honors in this critical department. One of these was a picture perfect performance at Laguna Seca; on the pole and leading every lap except two. His other wins were on the difficult Detroit course and at Mid-Ohio. He even scored an additional pair of poles.

Shrugging off a heartstopping crash at Fontana, from which he escaped essentially unhurt, he appears to have all the elements in place for a brilliant career at Marlboro Team Penske. The ebullience and good cheer he brings to the team is a remarkable contrast to the somber

2 Viva Mexico, national hero **ADRIAN FERNANDEZ** captained a driving lineup that made Patrick Racing the best two car team of 2000. He gets his own well financed team in 2001, a career long goal realized. (158 CART/FedEx Championship Series points)

~ Dan Bianchi

tones of 1999. Perhaps a better indicator of his caliber than his seventh place in the year's points standings is that only Juan Montoya led more laps in 2000.

2000 was a banner year, not for Michael Andretti, but for the infamous Andretti luck, which is mostly bad. The Andretti skills that made him the winningest active Champ Car driver with 38 victories at the end of 1999 were as polished as ever, but were tarnished by a couple of early season engine fires. Despite the setbacks, he won in Japan and again at Toronto, a circuit he likes. The victory plus a string of high level finishes put him at the top of the points chart just past midseason. At that juncture negotiations on contract renewal with Newman-Haas failed to reach fruition and he accepted a long term contract starting in 2001 with an arm of Team Green, backed by Motorola. In Australia, another engine fire took him out of the running for the title. He scored only two points in the last seven races of the year. Despite the DNFs, Andretti ran 290 laps in the lead, the year's third highest total and certainly merited a higher year end ranking than eighth. If Michael was deserving of better than his eighth slot for the year, Juan Montoya was certainly deserving of better than *his* ninth place. The 1999 champion was far and away the year's best pole producer with seven. He tied for first place in victories with three and ran more than twice as many laps in front (820) as next best Helio Castroneves. What he didn't do was finish often enough. Of the 12 times he failed to finish, 10 involved engine reliability; only the other two could be even partially laid at his door. He provided Toyota with its first ever CART victory on Milwaukee's flat oval and beat Michael Andretti in the year's best race, a 500 mile classic at Michigan. While there was no repeat FedEx Championship for Montoya, he goes back to drive in Formula One in 2001, a circuit on which he once toiled as a test driver.

Tenth place Cristiano da Matta made the record books in 2000, not only as a first time winner, but as the second driver to score using Toyota power. He showed such promise that

Carl Haas nominated him to take the place of departing star Michael Andretti in 2001. Certainly da Matta has star potential. In 1999, he occasionally contested the lead with eventual champion Juan Montoya, who presumably had a better mechanical package. With Newman-Haas he'll have the facilities to reach another level.

Still winless, 11th place Patrick Carpentier had the best year of his career with Player's Forsythe Racing eventhough sidelined for three races with a broken wrist, incurred in a fall at home. He also had a somewhat uncomfortable second half of the year during which he had no assurance that he'd be back for 2001. Post-season he was offered, and accepted a renewal. His best finish was at Gateway where he netted runner-up and fastest lap honors.

Twelfth place Christian Fittipaldi scored better at the payout window than the points chart. His single victory, in the season ending Marlboro 500, carried with it a $1 million bonus. Aside from the big win, he had only two podium placements, third at Portland and Mid-Ohio. With Michael Andretti gone, Fittipaldi will be the clear number one at Newman-Haas in 2001.

The year 2000 looked to be a great one for Max Papis. His first CART win came through in the season opening Homestead round. After that the promise went unfulfilled. He registered an unenviable 10 DNFs, made the podium only once more with second in Detroit. As a result he slipped nine places to 14th in the championship totals. To say he's looking for better things in 2001 would be a clear understatement.

On his graduation to the FedEx Championship ranks from Dayton Indy Lights, where he was the 1999 champion, Oriol Servia underwent a seeming character change. Previously noted for conservation, he became one of the chargers of 2000, regularly attempting and making daring passes. Not always, however, in Australia, he knocked Paul Tracy off course earning a $20,000 fine from CART and loss of his race points. His best finish was third in Detroit. Despite an attention-getting rookie

year he may be sidelined in 2001 since his PPI team has an uncertain future.

Gerry Forsythe's rookie find, Alex Tagliani, played a great opening act, and might even have won his first FedEx Championship race but the year's results were less than spectacular. He ended the season in the wall at Fontana and in 16th place for the year. At Homestead, he qualified fourth fastest and was leading when a pit lane violation dropped him to ninth. On the pole in Rio, his third start, he led for a long stretch, but a spin while in command cost him the victory. Fourth was his best race finish and 16th his rank at year end.

Mauricio Gugelmin and his PacWest team were saddled with an uncompetitive Mercedes engine but soldiered on and just missed the win at Nazareth. That would be his and Mercedes' only podium placement of the year in which he finished 17th on the leader board.

Relegated to a substitute role when his original Forsythe Championship team was withdrawn in a franchise dispute with CART, Bryan Herta did manage to get in six races with three different teams: Walker Racing, Mo Nunn and lastly Forsythe. For Forsythe he produced his best result, fourth on the grid and a fourth place finish on the track where he won the two previous year's races from the pole, Laguna Seca. He was 18th for the year.

Tony Kanaan, a winner in 1999, failed to make victory circle in 2000 with the new Mercedes powered Mo Nunn team. A qualifying crash in Detroit sidelined him for four races. He led at Nazareth and Homestead where he finished both in the top 10, contributing to his 19th place ranking for the year.

Memo Gidley had a two team year in 2000; three races for Player's Forsythe where he showed speed in the team's Reynard Honda substituting for Patrick Carpentier plus nine for Della Penna. At Della Penna he picked up points in his first four races, but none in the last five. He ranked 20th for the year and appears to be facing another season as a substitute in 2001.

Dan Bianchi

3 No longer super sub, just super, **ROBERTO MORENO** proved that with first class equipment and a full-time ride he could be a winner. He led the title chase for a while, was in it til the end. (147 CART/FedEx Championship Series points)

Ken Hawking

4 No beginner, but Rookie of the Year, **KENNY BRÄCK**, the 1998 Indianapolis 500 victor, did everything for team owner Bobby Rahal but win a race in his first CART season. (135 CART/FedEx Championship Series points)

5 Keeping his cool, Team KOOL Green stalwart **PAUL TRACY** won three races, combining his talent with discipline and staying in the title chase til the end despite a string of DNFs. (134 CART/FedEx Championship Series points)

Dan Bianchi

Dan Bianchi

6 1996 champion **JIMMY VASSER** got back in the win column at Houston after a victory drought in 1999. Not renewed for 2001 by team owner Chip Ganassi, he landed with Patrick Racing for the upcoming season. (131 CART/FedEx Championship Series points)

Dan Bianchi

7 Spirit and speed. HELIO CASTRONEVES brought a youthful enthusiasm along with three victories and three poles to the new look Marlboro Team Penske. He'll be hard to stop in 2001. (129 CART/FedEx Championship Series points)

Dan Bianchi

8 Bad luck blues pursued **MICHAEL ANDRETTI** virtually all year. He won two races, could easily have won three more and a second title except for mechanical failures. His long tenure at Newman-Haas Racing ended, he moves to Team Green in 2001. (127 CART/FedEx Championship Series points)

Dan Bianchi

9 Fast as ever but no repeat title. 1999 champion **JUAN MONTOYA** won three races in 2000, as many as any other driver, led 820 laps, more than twice as many as any other driver. All this despite 12 DNFs, all but two mechanical. He goes back to Formula One in 2001, but will be missed. (126 CART/FedEx Championship Series points)

10 A winner on Toyota power, **CRISTIANO DA MATTA** exhibited flair and front running ability in cracking the year's top 10. His reward, a 2001 seat on the Newman-Haas team, second only to Marlboro Team Penske in total victories. (112 CART/FedEx Championship Series points)

Dan Bianchi

Cheryl Day Anderson

Dan Bianchi

11 **PATRICK CARPENTIER**'s best season ever despite missing three races with a broken wrist. Second place at Gateway was its high point. His return to Player's Forsythe Racing for 2001 was announced after the season ended. (101 CART/FedEx Championship Series points)

12 **CHRISTIAN FITTIPALDI** won the million dollar Marlboro bonus in the season ending event at Fontana. It was his only victory of the year but leaves him well poised for his sixth season with Newman-Haas in 2001. (96 CART/FedEx Championship points)

Dan Bianchi

13 **DARIO FRANCHITTI** had a reversal of fortune. The talented Team KOOL Green driver, almost the champion in 1999, failed to win in 2000. An accident in Spring training got him off to a slow start and he never matched his previous year's form. (92 CART/FedEx Championship Series points)

Dan Bianchi

14 A great start for **MAX PAPIS'** 2000 season was overshadowed by DNF gremlins. He won the opening Homestead event and then failed to finish in more than half the remaining races. He'll be back with Team Rahal in 2001, in a bid to turn things around. (88 CART/FedEx Championship points)

Ken Hawking

15 Role reversal for **ORIOL SERVIA**. Noted for conservatism in his 1999 Dayton Indy Lights Championship year he became a charger in his first CART season. His team, PPI Motorsports, may be on the sidelines in 2001 and he may be relegated to a substitute role. (60 CART/FedEx Championship Series points)

Dan Bianchi

16 **ALEX TAGLIANI**'s early promise will have to wait til 2001 for fulfillment. The prize Canadian rookie, on Gerry Forsythe's Player's Forsythe team, might have won his first race except for a pit violation. In his third race he was on the pole and the dominant driver but spun. No victories until 2001 at the earliest. (53 CART/FedEx Championship Series points)

Dan Bianchi

Cheryl Day Anderson

17 Mercedes powered PacWest veteran **MAURICIO GUGELMIN** produced a solid second place at Nazareth. That was the year's high point. PacWest will get new power in 2001. (39 CART/FedEx Championship Series points)

18 Sidelined by a franchise dispute, **BRYAN HERTA** picked up rides with three different teams. Best outing, for Gerry Forsythe, was fourth at Laguna Seca where he was the winner the two previous years. (26 CART/FedEx Championship Series points)

Ken Hawking

Dan Bianchi

19 A winner in 1999, **TONY KANAAN,** now with the Mercedes powered new Mo Nunn team, missed the mark widely in 2000. Both will have a new powerplant in 2001. (24 CART/FedEx Championship Series points)

20 Fate may send **MEMO GIDLEY** back to the substitute ranks in 2001. He performed well for Player's Forsythe, filling in for an injured Patrick Carpentier, and later as a full-time Della Penna Racing driver. (20 CART/FedEx Championship Series points)

FedEx Championship Series Race 1
Marlboro Grand Prix of Miami
Presented by Toyota
Homestead-Miami Speedway
March 26, 2000

MAX PAPIS MOVES INTO THE WINNERS' RANKS IN THE MARLBORO GRAND PRIX

Agonizingly close before, Max Papis moved into the winner's circle for the first time with a daring pass of Paul Tracy with 10 laps remaining in Homestead's Marlboro Grand Prix. Tracy had hustled his poor handling Team KOOL Green Reynard Honda into the lead from 17th place on the starting grid but was happy to salvage a podium position. Papis' pal and countryman Roberto Moreno also jumped on Tracy's troubles and garnered runner-up honors, his best ever CART oval finish. The big news in qualifying was that new look Marlboro Team Penske was back in form, back in style. New

driver Gil de Ferran nailed down the pole position and might have brought off the win except for an unfortunately timed pit stop that unceremoniously dropped him down to sixth at the checker. 1999 champion Juan Montoya dashed into the lead on the first lap from his front row starting slot and held it for 21 laps. He managed only two more circuits before his engine, Toyota this year, quit. Adrian Fernandez, the third fastest qualifier, then took over the top spot on the leader board for 25 laps before giving into mechanical problems. Kenny Bräck, Papis' teammate on the Bobby Rahal squad, had the heady experience of leading his first ever CART race for five laps before giving into mechanical problems. Jimmy Vasser had better luck than his Target Chip Ganassi teammate Montoya, starting 10th, finishing fourth. Player's Forsythe's Patrick Carpentier made a workmanlike move into fifth place from 12th on the grid. While he never led a lap, Michael Andretti was very much in contention, when his engine

gave up. Carpentier teammate, rookie fellow Canadian Alex Tagliani provided some of the day's most colorful moments. Fourth on the starting grid, he actually led a pair of laps before running afoul of the authorities for passing the pace car on a trip to the pits. After a penalty he still made it into the day's top 10 but he could have been in the countdown for the win. Marlboro Team Penske had another first, in addition to de Ferran's pole. Teammate Helio Castroneves was the first mechanical casualty of the day after qualifying in the top 10. Even this incident failed to dampen spirits in the Penske campaign headquarters. The Captain's men could sense that victory was getting closer on their screens instead of slipping further away as it did in 1998 and '99.

The top 10 in points after the event were: Max Papis, 20; Roberto Moreno, 16; Paul Tracy, 14; Jimmy Vasser, 12; Patrick Carpentier, 10; Gil de Ferran, 10; Christian Fittipaldi, 6; Shinji Nakano, 5; Alexandre Tagliani, 4 and Tony Kanaan, 3.

Steve Swope

FedEx Championship Series Race 2
Toyota Grand Prix of Long Beach
Streets of Long Beach, CA
April 16, 2000

PAUL TRACY TAKES THE TOYOTA GRAND PRIX OF LONG BEACH FROM FAR BACK IN THE FIELD

For the second time in a row, Paul Tracy's Team KOOL Green group couldn't get the set up right for qualifying, saddling their star driver with a 17th place on the starting grid. This time they did get it right by race time and Tracy responded with a masterful drive that saw him in the lead for the last 20 laps. He was a handsome 3.191 seconds ahead of Marlboro Team Penske recruit Helio Castroneves at the finish. Gil de Ferran again demonstrated the Penske contingent's new muscle by capturing his second pole in a row and leading the first 30 laps. He finished fourth after two bumping incidents. Jimmy Vasser had a good day, outqualifying teammate Juan Montoya in second place, and finishing third. Montoya failed to lead a single lap and again dropped out with mechanical maladies. Rookie Alexandre "Tag" Tagliani continued to demonstrate a high turn of speed with 11th place on the starting grid and a fourth place finish. Bryan Herta, filling in for an injured Shinji Nakano at Walker Racing, produced a solid fifth place finish, on top of a fifth fastest qualifying time. Michael Andretti got in 12 lead laps midway but lost out to an engine fire. 1999 Dayton Indy Lights champion Oriol Servia, driving for PPI Motorsports, scored a useful sixth place. After the event, staged in front of a crowd estimated at 100,000, Tracy led the points parade, but Marlboro Team Penske had demonstrated speed capable of being converted into victory.

FedEx Championship Series Race 3
Rio 200
Emerson Fittipaldi Speedway
at Nelson Piquet International Raceway
Rio de Janeiro, Brazil
April 30, 2000

ROOKIE ALEX TAGLIANI SPINS, VETERAN ADRIAN FERNANDEZ SNAPS UP THE RIO 200 VICTORY

The scenario sounded too good to be true, and as it played out it was too good to be true. With only nine laps to go, Player's Forsythe rookie Alex Tagliani was leading, as he had been most of the afternoon from his starting slot on the pole. Victory in only his third FedEx Championship start was clearly in sight. Then he spun and wily veteran Adrian Fernandez slipped by into the lead. Tagliani then repeated the spin procedure, allowing Fernandez the win under yellow. The crestfallen rookie ended up 13th. Fernandez ended up in victory circle, with plaudits for his Firestone tires which allowed him to make two tire pit stops en route to overcoming a 16th place starting position. Fernandez's closest pursuer across the finish line was Jimmy Vasser, the runner-up, with whom he dueled all day. Paul Tracy qualified third, finished third, despite encounters with Max Papis and the gyrating Tagliani. Overcoming mechanical problems in qualifying, Cristiano da Matta climbed up the leader board to a fourth place finish from a lackluster 17th place starting slot. Christian Fittipaldi qualified fifth fastest, finished fifth after overcoming a slow pit stop. Michael Andretti managed a lap in the lead but spoiled his chances by hitting two crew members on a pit stop and incurring a stop-and-go penalty. He finished ninth. 1999 champion Juan Montoya was the second fastest qualifier and the only driver to keep Tagliani in sight - until he was sidelined again with mechanical problems.

FedEx Championship Series Race 4
Firestone Firehawk 500
Twin Ring Motegi
Motegi, Japan
May 13, 2000

LUCKY AT LAST, MICHAEL ANDRETTI BAGS HIS 39TH CHAMP CAR WIN AT MOTEGI

Undeterred by a rain postponement, Juan Montoya snatched the pole, added a dominating drive but ended up in seventh place at the finish. Chief beneficiary of a botched Montoya pit stop, and winner of the Firestone Firehawk 500 was Michael Andretti, whose luck in the year's first two outings had been abysmal. He inherited the lead when Montoya had to make an extra, fifth pit stop and cruised to victory with a .546 second cushion over Dario Franchitti. Franchitti had an indifferent starting slot, 17th, but showing his 1999 form, got by Roberto Moreno late in the race, to earn runner-up honors, his best showing of 2000. After running in the top half dozen all day, Moreno held on for the third podium position. Showing speed and tenacity, Cristiano da Matta, the top Toyota powered finisher, managed a fourth place finish from 19th on the starting grid. Fast in practice and second fastest in qualifying, Kenny Bräck struggled with handling problems during the race to notch the final top five finishing position. Also beset by handling problems, Paul Tracy soldiered on to a sixth place finish, in so doing retained his points lead over Jimmy Vasser and Roberto Moreno. After four events the championship points leader board showed Paul Tracy, 56; Vasser and Moreno at 42; Max Papis and Cristiano da Matta at 25.

SNOW FAILS TO STOP GIL DE FERRAN EN ROUTE TO ROGER PENSKE'S 100th VICTORY

It should have taken place early in April but actually ran late in May, due to snow on Sunday and temperatures too low for tire safety on Monday. Nazareth's Bosch Spark Plug Grand Prix nonetheless was a happy occasion for Marlboro Team Penske and star driver Gil de Ferran who pulled off his first win in the employ of Roger Penske. It was Penske's 100th, which had been three years in coming. It was "just a matter of time," noted de Ferran who had won the pole in the year's first two outings but couldn't convert the advantage to victory. Surprise runner-up Mauricio Gugelmin, in the year's best finish for a Mercedes powered driver, was among the first to congratulate de Ferran and his team. Kenny Bräck, having earlier proven he could run up front, posted his first podium finish of the year in third place after starting sixth. Juan Montoya was on the pole and the race's preeminent driver with more than half the laps in the lead. An extra pit stop to repair collision damage cost him the victory. He finished fourth. It was a day of fives for Adrian Fernandez. Fifth on the starting grid, fifth at the finish, and a move up to fifth place in the season's points totals. It was not a great day for hometown favorite Michael Andretti. He started back in 15th place, had a car that was never quite right, and still managed a sixth place finish. De Ferran's win was strictly on merit. He led the last 68 laps for a .815 second margin of victory.

The top 10 in the points chase following the Bosch Spark Plug Grand Prix were: Paul Tracy, 59; Jimmy Vasser, 48; Gil de Ferran, 42; Roberto Moreno, 42; Adrian Fernandez, 33; Michael Andretti, 28; Kenny Bräck, 27; Max Papis, 25; Cristiano da Matta, 25 and Juan Montoya, 22.

Steve Swope

Steve Swope

Juan Montoya gets Toyota its first Champ Car victory in the Miller Lite 225 at The Milwaukee Mile

FedEx Championship Series Race 6
Miller Lite 225
The Milwaukee Mile
June 5, 2000

JUAN MONTOYA TURNS THE MILLER LITE 225 INTO TOYOTA'S FIRST CHAMP CAR VICTORY

With seven wins in 1999, reigning champion Juan Montoya was no stranger to victory lane, but his first victory of 2000 also set another landmark, the first ever for Toyota in the FedEx Championship Series. For the third time this year Montoya, in his Target Ganassi Lola Toyota, was on the pole. This time no nasty mechanical problems intervened en route to a rain postponed victory. On the venerable Milwaukee Mile he led 179 laps of the 225 total, including the last 38. He had a 1.015 second cushion over runner-up Michael Andretti whose car co-owner, Carl Haas, promoted the race. Andretti was the only driver able to put any pressure on Montoya all afternoon. Player's Forsythe driver Patrick Carpentier had an upbeat day. He qualified third, put some heat on Montoya in the early going and finished third. Fourth place Kenny Bräck led for seven laps but lost his chance at a podium finish when he stalled while in the pits. Fifth place finisher Roberto Moreno also enjoyed some laps in the lead (23) up from a seventh place start but was not a factor in the final countdown. Second fastest qualifier Dario Franchitti was unable to maintain that level in the race. He finished sixth. Toyota's Racing Manager Les Unger said it all, "an awesome day for Toyota."

After the Miller Lite 225 the top 10 in the points were Paul Tracy, 59; Roberto Moreno, 52; Jimmy Vasser, 48; Michael Andretti, 44; Juan Montoya, 44; Gil de Ferran, 43; Kenny Bräck, 43; Adrian Fernandez, 38; Max Papis, 31 and Dario Franchitti, 28.

FedEx Championship Series Race 7
Tenneco Automotive Grand Prix of Detroit
The Raceway on Belle Isle
June 18, 2000

PENSKE PICK HELIO CASTRONEVES TAMES THE TOUGH BELLE ISLE CIRCUIT FOR HIS FIRST VICTORY

Only a third of the way into the 2000 season, brash young Helio Castroneves proved the wisdom of his selection as the second driver on a totally reorganized Marlboro Team Penske. The young Brazilian joined countryman teammate Gil de Ferran as a winner, by taking the Tenneco Automotive Grand Prix of Detroit. He qualified third and inherited the lead when track record setting polesitter Juan Montoya limped to the sidelines with drivetrain failure. Montoya had led every one of the first 60 laps but ended up with another dismal DNF as his reward. Max Papis, the second fastest qualifier was no match for Montoya - or Castroneves, who enjoyed a huge 4.415 second margin of victory, but drove a smart, "no mistakes" race good for second place. 1999 Dayton Indy Lights champion Oriol Servia abandoned his conservative tactics of last year to charge up from 12th on the starting grid to a podium position, his first, at the end, in the Telefonica Reynard Toyota. Team KOOL Green's Dario Franchitti matched Montoya's qualifying time and started second. He almost lost it, trying to beat Target-Ganassi's Montoya into the first turn at the start and ended up in fourth place. Back in action for Player's Forsythe, Patrick Carpentier had to favor his still recovering broken wrist, but produced a workmanlike fifth place finish from ninth on the starting grid. Rookie teammate Alex Tagliani produced no fireworks this time, only a respectable sixth place finish. Seventh place in the race helped Jimmy Vasser pick up some ground on points leader Paul Tracy who was black flagged for a pit row encounter with one of his crew members. The day's proceedings proved that Marlboro Team Penske, now with two winners in its stable, is well launched on its campaign for the second 100 victories.

Cheryl Day Anderson

Steve Swope

FedEx Championship Series Race 8
Freightliner/G.I. Joe's 200
Presented by Texaco
Portland International Raceway
June 25, 2000

GIL DE FERRAN GRABS HIS SECOND VICTORY OF THE YEAR AT PORTLAND

Young pole winner Helio Castroneves got all the attention through the first 100 laps of the race but teammate Gil de Ferran walked off with top honors. De Ferran started on the front row but at times was as much as five seconds behind the "junior" member of his team. A failed fueling strategy that involved a late race "splash-and-go" stop that didn't have enough "splash" required an additional stop. That cost Castroneves the win and demoted him to seventh place at the end. By contrast, de Ferran had plenty of fuel and built up a huge margin in the closing stages. He was a handsome 2.625 seconds ahead of runner-up Roberto Moreno at the finish. Moreno, the third fastest qualifier, felt he was balked by an about to be lapped Patrick Carpentier when he was trying to get around and close in on de Ferran. Newman-Haas teammates Christian Fittipaldi and Michael Andretti notched the third and fourth positions in useful rides without drama except Andretti's encounter with Luiz Garcia in the process of passing. Sixth finisher Kenny Bräck clocked the race's fastest lap in the process of recovering from a mild tangle with Dario Franchitti. Moreno's runner-up points vaulted him to the top of the points chart with 68. De Ferran's 20 points made him runner-up with 67 followed by Tracy, 59; Andretti, 56 and Vasser 54.

FedEx Championship Series Race 9
Marconi Grand Prix of Cleveland
Presented by Firstar
Burke Lakefront Airport
July 2, 2000

ROBERTO MORENO MAKES MARCONI GRAND PRIX OF CLEVELAND INTO HIS BIGGEST DAY

What more could a much traveled ex-substitute driver want than his first pole and his first victory in the FedEx Championship all on the same day. Not much, as Roberto Moreno noted in his post-race comments. "It's been a long time trying to find the right ride at the right time." He is now happily ensconced with Patrick Racing and, with first rate equipment on a full time basis, he's making his presence felt on the circuit. With second fastest qualifier Gil de Ferran having a bad day due to brake failure, Moreno now leads the championship parade by 32 points over Michael Andretti. From an unimposing 15th place on the starting grid Kenny Bräck battled his way up the leader board to claim runner-up honors. Bumped at the start and demoted 10 places from his fifth position on the starting grid. Cristiano da Matta performed admirably to notch the third podium position. Michael Andretti qualified fourth fastest, got as high as second but had to settle for fourth place at the checker. Patrick Carpentier earned the Budweiser "Hard Charger" award for his feat of moving from 19th at the start to top five status at the finish. Juan Montoya was sixth on the starting grid but went wide in a first lap, first turn multi-car mix up. He recovered to set the fastest race lap but seventh place at the finish was as far forward as he was able to get. Moreno essentially owned the day. He led the first 33 laps and the last 57 and got through the first turn cleanly, ahead of the big tangle that affected so many pursuers.

Steve Swope

FedEx Championship Series Race 10
Molson Indy
Toronto Street Course
July 15, 2000

**MICHAEL ANDRETTI
MAKES THE MOLSON INDY
HIS 40th CHAMP CAR WIN**

Short of their own Canadian drivers, Toronto fans love Michael Andretti, CART's winningest active pilot returns the favor. He has now won here six times, more than he has on any other circuit. His latest victory raised his career total to 40, and no other driver appears close to catching him. Although Andretti led the last 32 laps and had a huge 6.527 second cushion over runner-up Adrian Fernandez at the end, it took him a while to get up front. The early going belonged to Cristiano da Matta who beat pole winner Helio Castroneves into the first turn and headed the pack for the first 73 laps. Andretti then registered a single circuit in front before giving way to the Patrick pair of Adrian Fernandez and Roberto Moreno who were, as they often did, getting better fuel mileage from their Fords. After their stops, Andretti regained the lead for good.

As noted, Fernandez held on for second place but Moreno dropped out with gearbox problems. Cheered on by his countrymen, Paul Tracy passed a fading da Matta for the final podium spot. Unlucky pole winner Castroneves encountered mechanical problems and dropped out. Canadian rookie Alex Tagliani notched the last top five position in a rousing drive from 19th on the grid. Points leader Roberto Moreno (90) had gearbox problems and also dropped out enabling Andretti (88) to move up to within two points of the top spot. In addition to liking the circuit, Andretti noted that he liked the city and its fans. He should.

FedEx Championship Series Race 11
Michigan 500
Michigan Speedway
July 23, 2000

THE YEAR'S BEST RACE GOES TO JUAN MONTOYA OVER MICHAEL ANDRETTI

Separated by only .04 second at the checker, after 15 lead swapping final laps at Michigan, Juan Montoya and Michael Andretti were the lead players in a drama that had Michigan fans out of their seats and cheering. Andretti had a slight lead on the final lap when bit player Tarso Marques entered the stage. He went high to give the two flying leaders room. Montoya went with him, got enough draft to get past Andretti, who took the conventional low route. Consolation prize for Andretti was the points leadership at 104, ahead of previous leader Roberto Moreno who dropped out of today's race early with gearbox problems. Dario Franchitti claimed third place from fourth on the grid, with teammate and pole winner Paul Tracy notching seventh place. Patrick Carpentier had another solid points paying finish in fourth place. The last top five placement went to Helio Castroneves who earned the most laps led point with 85. Adrian Fernandez matched his sixth place race finish with his sixth place standing on the lap leader board. While 10 different drivers managed to get at least one lap in the lead, the afternoon belonged to Montoya and Andretti and their excitement charged 15 lap duel at speeds in excess of 230 miles per hour.

Following the Michigan 500 the top five in the points chase were: Roberto Moreno, 90; Michael Andretti, 88; Gil de Ferran, 75; Paul Tracy, 73; Kenny Bräck, 66.

Steve Swope

FedEx Championship Series Race 12
TARGET Grand Prix
Presented by Energizer
Chicago Motor Speedway
July 30, 2000

CRISTIANO DA MATTA SCORES HIS BREAK-THROUGH FIRST VICTORY AT CHICAGO

Target/Chip Ganassi's pole winner Juan Montoya wanted to hand his boss Chip Ganassi the victory at Ganassi's Chicago Motor Speedway just as he had last year. He ended up stalled on the straight with electrical problems after dominating the race through the first 170 laps. Cristiano da Matta just wanted to collect his first Champ Car victory anywhere and, he did just that - in style. En route to the winner's circle he had to get by a consistently quick Kenny Bräck who had two sessions in the lead and fight off a fast closing Michael Andretti. He accomplished both tasks with finesse, leading the last 50 laps and crossing the finish line 1.69 seconds ahead of runner-up Andretti. In one of his typical stealth attacks, Gil de Ferran snuck into third place, ahead of Bräck who finished just where he started, fourth. Adrian Fernandez nailed down the last slot in the top five. Not only was the win a personal triumph for da Matta, it was a banner day for his PPI Motorsports team, which had been in the Toyota camp since its early days in 1996. Roberto Moreno managed sixth place, the last runner on the lead lap. Mauricio Gugelmin finished seventh down a lap. Though denied the victory, Andretti enhanced his lead in the FedEx Championship Series points with a total of 120. Moreno, 98; de Ferran, 89; da Matta, 82 and Tracy, 80 completed the top five.

FedEx Championship Series Race 13
Miller Lite 200
Mid-Ohio Sports Car Course
August 13, 2000

MARLBORO TEAM PENSKE ROMPS AT MID-OHIO, HELIO CASTRONEVES & GIL DE FERRAN SCORE A 1-2 FINISH

Gil de Ferran was on the pole, teammate Helio Castroneves alongside him on the front row at the start of the Miller Lite 200. De Ferran scooted off in the lead, held it for the first 28 laps with Castroneves in tow. Castroneves had the better pit stop and reeled off the final 55 laps.

He was a full 4.425 seconds ahead of de Ferran at the finish. Nobody else came close to the red and white pair of flying Honda powered Reynskes, as insiders call the much modified Penske Reynards, which seem to have a clear edge on road courses. Closest, but never a threat, was Newman-Haas' Christian Fittipaldi, courageously returning to the fray after a huge practice shunt at Chicago that kept him out of action for two events. Max Papis qualified sixth fastest, picked up one place at the start and another with a well-timed pit stop to finish fourth. Kenny Bräck was the fourth fastest qualifier, traded places with Dario Franchitti, third on the starting grid, early in the event,

would have finished third except for an overly lengthy pit stop. Franchitti was competitive early in the race, keeping the Penske pair in sight, but lost two laps to electrical problems and eventually retired after tagging Jimmy Vasser. Adrian Fernandez, who started 12th, used great fuel mileage advantageously to finish sixth. Reigning champion Juan Montoya endured a dismal day. After his worst qualifying effort of the year he slithered off course twice and later ran out of fuel, to register his eighth DNF of the season. As the season progresses it is becoming increasingly clear that the Penske forces have massaged their Reynards into this year's prize mechanical package.

Steve Swope

Steve Swope

FedEx Championship Series Race 14
Motorola 220
Road America
August 20, 2000

PAUL TRACY PREVAILS IN THE MOTOROLA 220 FROM THE BACK OF THE PACK

To the delight of a large, partisan crowd, Canadian Paul Tracy won the Molson Indy Vancouver, the second Canadian stop in the wide ranging FedEx Championship Series. Tracy's teammate, polesitter and leader for the first 40 laps, Dario Franchitti would likely have been the victor had he not stalled in the pits on his second and final stop. Since this pair had an unhappy history of tangling late in the race and giv-ing away almost certain wins, team orders to stay in line after the last pit stop unless threatened by competi-tors were in effect. Franchitti accepted his runner-up position on the podium in good grace, despite the fact that he had yet to win in 2000 and Tracy had already won twice. Tracy, the second fastest qualifier admitted that Franchitti had the faster car, but had no choice but to run out the last 37 laps to the end. The only other driver

FedEx Championship Series Race 15
Molson Indy Vancouver
Concord Pacific Place
September 3, 2000

CANADIAN PAUL TRACY MASTERS THE MOLSON INDY VANCOUVER

"I don't know how we did it," admitted Paul Tracy after winning Road America's Motorola 220. Just after the start his Honda engine cut out. Keeping his cool, which an earlier edition Paul Tracy might not have done, he followed radio instructions from Team KOOL Green engineer Tony Cicale. Miraculously his engine fired up again, but he was mired in the back of the pack. Tracy stayed focused on the huge challenge ahead and picked off his opponents, one by one. Admittedly only 15 of the 25 starters were running at the finish, but Tracy's accomplishment was still monumental. He was an unbelievable 7.450 seconds ahead of runner-up Adrian Fernandez at the finish. Kenny Bräck had sparred with Fernandez all afternoon and followed him across the line in third place. The early going featured a great dice between Juan Montoya and rookie Alex Tagliani who shared the lead. Montoya's gearbox collapsed on lap 30, leaving Tagliani looking like a winner until *his* gearbox went, seven laps later. This sequence of events, coupled with a focused and flying Tracy, put the Team KOOL Green driver in front for the first time. Fernandez and Moreno, the fourth place finisher, each had a brief run in the lead, but the final five laps belonged to Tracy. Pole winner Dario Franchitti, who never managed a lead lap, was another gearbox victim, after 43 laps. A consistent Jimmy Vasser checked in for the last spot in the top five. Sixth place Memo Gidley and seventh place Max Papis were the only other runners to finish on the lead lap. Tracy's triumph was his 17th in the FedEx Championship Series and perhaps his most satisfying.

to poke a nose out in front was Gil de Ferran who posted two laps in the lead. He finished fifth. A consistent Adrian Fernandez occupied the third podium position, largely on the basis of a clever pit strategy. Attrition helped sixth fastest qualifier Christian Fittipaldi move up to fourth at the end. Jimmy Vasser was the beneficiary of some fast pit work in moving from 11th at the start to sixth at the finish. Seventh finisher Cristiano da Matta made a failed attempt to go the distance on one stop but had to scurry in for a splash-and-go. While Tracy's third win of the year was at his teammate's expense, he ran a fast, clean race, enabling him to gain on points leader Michael Andretti who suffered another painful DNF with fuel pressure problems. The points leaders at this stage were: Andretti, 125; Moreno, 112; de Ferran, 106; Fernandez, 103; Bräck, 102 and Tracy, 100.

ANOTHER 1-2 FINISH FOR MARLBORO TEAM PENSKE, HELIO CASTRONEVES & GIL DE FERRAN REIGN AT LAGUNA SECA

What a fitting present to hand race sponsor Honda; a one-two finish in the Honda Grand Prix of Monterey. Honda engines have been very good to Marlboro Team Penske in 2000; as of today, power for five victories and, in the person of driver Gil de Ferran, first place in the point standings with the season three-quarters complete. Young charger Helio Castroneves established himself as a ranking star by capturing the pole and leading every lap save two that went to 1999 champion Juan Montoya. Montoya's chances were marred by an air jack problem on his second pit stop, and he was relegated to a sixth place finish. The elder statesman of the Penske pair, Gil de Ferran, ran second virtually all afternoon, claiming runner-up honors .954 seconds behind Castroneves. Dario Franchitti qualified third fastest, finished third in a workmanlike race. Forsythe Championship Racing fielded a Reynard Ford for Bryan Herta, winner of the two previous year's events here. He qualified fourth, finished in the same slot. Sixth fastest qualifier Kenny Bräck gained fifth place at the finish, on the basis of a quicker pit stop. A two fuel stop strategy for nearly the entire field, dictated an economy mode rather than all out combat.

Steve Swope

MOTOROLA 300 GOES TO JUAN MONTOYA AFTER MICHAEL ANDRETTI EXITS

Michael Andretti won last year's Motorola 300 with a combination of heads up driving and heads up pit work. He owned this year's edition, having lapped the entire field except for pole winner Juan Montoya until his engine expired with 40 laps to go. Andretti's misfortune, "just snakebitten, I guess," was how he phrased it, handed the win to Montoya. Once Andretti took over the lead on lap 67 there was no question who was in command, until his dismal departure. An on form Patrick Carpentier qualified fifth fastest, led briefly on pit stops and inherited runner-up honors. Roberto Moreno moved up steadily from a mid-pack start to claim the third podium position and move up in the points chase with a 129 total on leader Gil de Ferran (137). Cristiano da Matta, started in 10th place, progressed through the pack to a fourth place finish. Rookie Oriol Servia, who qualified only 18th fastest, executed a series of daring passes to nail down the final rung in the day's top five.

Jimmy Vasser leads the pack at the
Texaco/Havoline Grand Prix of Houston

FedEx Championship Series Race 18
Texaco/Havoline Grand Prix of Houston
Streets of Houston
October 1, 2000

JIMMY VASSER TAKES THE TEXACO/HAVOLINE GRAND PRIX OF HOUSTON

1996 champion Jimmy Vasser's 2000 employment prospects got a bit brighter when he won a clear cut victory on Houston's street circuit, his first in over a year and a half. Already notified by team owner Chip Ganassi that his services weren't required next year, Vasser got added satisfaction by beating his brilliant teammate Juan Montoya in the bargain. Runner-up Montoya was 1.914 second behind at the finish. Points leader Gil de Ferran led the first 46 laps, building up a huge cushion but was forced to make a second quick pit stop for fuel, whereas Vasser went the distance on a single stop. De Ferran is too intelligent to take a chance on running out of fuel, knowing that the 14 points that accompanied his third place today would serve him well in the championship chase he leads.

Winner here last year, Team KOOL Green's Paul Tracy never got higher than fourth place today, his finishing status. Tracy teammate Dario Franchitti, the 1999 runner-up here and second fastest qualifier, got off to a bad start and crashed on only his second lap. Helio Castroneves ran as high as third place early in the proceedings, suffered a lengthy pit stop and recouped to finish fifth. Michael Andretti suffered a series of mishaps, a stalled engine in the pits and a big shunt from rookie Alex Tagliani, His 13th place, corresponding to his luck in 2000, put a damper on his championship hopes. Teammate Christian Fittipaldi had an uneventful outing that ended in seventh place.

FedEx Championship Series Race 19
Honda Indy 300
Gold Coast, Queensland, Australia
October 15, 2000

ADRIAN FERNANDEZ HAULS IN THE HONDA INDY 300 LAURELS, AFTER THE LEADERS CRASH

Juan Montoya, Gil de Ferran and Dario Franchitti were the three fastest qualifiers - and the first three to become spectators in a wild scenario at the Honda Indy 300. De Ferran and Montoya crashed in the first turn of the first lap and were eliminated. Franchitti was caught up in the tangle and got punted by Jimmy Vasser. He completed only a single lap. This bizarre beginning turned over the lead to Paul Tracy, who then was stricken with a stuck throttle. He recovered only to be bumped out of the race, and for all practical purposes, out of the championship chase by rookie Oriol Servia in a failed passing attempt. The Team KOOL Green stalwart was understandably upset. Jimmy Vasser, Kenny Bräck and Alex Tagliani all posted stints in the lead. Then on lap 43, Adrian Fernandez, in one of his patented sneak attacks, emerged from the obscurity of his 17th place on the starting grid to take the lead, quietly but firmly. He reeled off the remaining 16 laps in front to edge Bräck by 0.324 seconds at the finish. Third place Jimmy Vasser captured the texture of the event in his post-race observation, "There was a lot of crazy driving out there today." Fourth place went to Cristiano da Matta who was happy just to finish, fifth to Patrick Carpentier. De Ferran could have wrapped up the FedEx Series Driver's Championship today. Instead, he'll have to contend with Fernandez, who is now only five points behind, in the Fontana finale. Tracy and Bräck, with 19 point deficits, are also still in the running. Vasser and Moreno, 22 points behind, remain theoretical title candidates but their odds are slim indeed. Michael Andretti, the mid-season points leader, is out of contention.

Steve Swope

Steve Swope

FedEx Championship Series Race 20
Marlboro 500 Presented by Toyota
California Speedway
October 30, 2000

MARLBORO'S MILLION DOLLAR WINNER'S BONUS GOES TO CHRISTIAN FITTIPALDI

GIL DE FERRAN TAKES THE FEDEX CHAMPIONSHIP SERIES

Christian Fittipaldi won an attrition marked Marlboro 500 in which there were only six finishers. All except Gil de Ferran's third place Honda were on Ford power. "Ultra conservative" is how new champion de Ferran characterized his race. He was on the pole with a new world closed course record of 241.428 mph and could have gone much faster. However, any faster might have cost him the championship and de Ferran is too intelligent to take that risk. His closest pursuer in the championship, Adrian Fernandez, was almost eight mph slower in qualifying. Fernandez was never a threat to de Ferran during the event. He finished fifth on the day and second in the championship.

Newman-Haas teammates Michael Andretti and Fittipaldi qualified next fastest after de Ferran. Andretti was the first of the pair to take the lead. He was running fifth when he encountered blinding smoke from Tony Kanaan's blown engine and tangled with Oriol Servia in a fitting end to an unlucky season.

Fittipaldi first took the lead on lap 138, regained it on lap 222 and held on for his first victory of the year, the second of his career. In an unusual move, the first 33 laps of the event on Sunday, before rain halted racing, counted when it was resumed on Monday in front of a diminished audience. Roberto Moreno, who evaded all the lurking mechanical gremlins that abounded on the day, came through to a handsome second place, notching third place in the championship chase. The surprise fourth place finisher was young Casey Mears, a Dayton Indy Lights standout, who was given a one-off ride by Bobby Rahal. In gratitude he kept out of trouble, conserved his machinery and finished on the lead lap for a very respectable first Champ Car drive. Seventh place Tarso Marques was the only other finisher although he was placed behind Alex Tagliani who spun

in his own oil and banged the wall hard enough to require a hospital trip. The same fate befell Helio Castroneves who had multiple turns in the lead before his accident. Juan Montoya, in his farewell CART appearance before joining the Formula One circuit in 2001, was leading the race when it was stopped on Sunday. He led again on Monday but joined the spectator contingent when his engine gave up on lap 219. Except for the understandable joy in the Marlboro Team Penske campaign headquarters at their swift return to championship status, it was an understated ending to an exciting, competitive season. Ford, too, had cause to celebrate. Today's strong finish gave them the Manufacturer's Championship.

2000 CART MANUFACTURER'S CHAMPIONSHIP	
FORD	335
HONDA	313
TOYOTA	275
MERCEDES	74

EuroSpeedway, Lausitzring, Germany

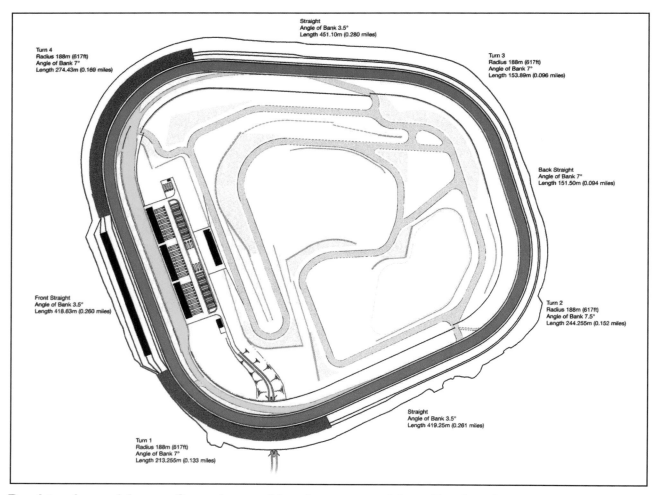

Straight
Angle of Bank 3.5°
Length 451.10m (0.280 miles)

Turn 4
Radius 188m (617ft)
Angle of Bank 7°
Length 274.43m (0.169 miles)

Turn 3
Radius 188m (617ft)
Angle of Bank 7°
Length 153.89m (0.096 miles)

Back Straight
Angle of Bank 7°
Length 151.50m (0.094 miles)

Front Straight
Angle of Bank 3.5°
Length 418.63m (0.260 miles)

Turn 2
Radius 188m (617ft)
Angle of Bank 7.5°
Length 244.255m (0.152 miles)

Straight
Angle of Bank 3.5°
Length 419.25m (0.261 miles)

Turn 1
Radius 188m (617ft)
Angle of Bank 7°
Length 213.255m (0.133 miles)

Rockingham Motor Speedway, Northamptonshire, England

Fundidora Park, Monterrey, Mexico

Three New Venues
Two In Europe, One In Mexico, Spice CART's 2001 Calendar

Champ Car racing and Champ Car drivers are not totally new to Europe but the last outing was in 1978 and not on a purpose built American style oval. Now there are two new multimillion dollar ovals with firm CART dates on the 2001 schedule. First up, on September 15, is Germany's Eurospeedway, familiarly known as the Lausitzring, a 2.0 mile tri-oval, with a 4.5 mile infield road circuit and a separate 3.5 mile testing facility. It cost approximately $120 million and is positioned between Dresden and Berlin. Hans-Jorg Fischer, the CEO, is confident that oval track racing with Champ Cars will be popular because of its previous television exposure and the fact that spectators can see a lot more than a single corner or straight.

Next up, on September 22, is Rockingham Motor Speedway in Corby, Northamptonshire, England, just 70 miles from London and strate-gically positioned between three major motorways. Within a hundred miles of the $75 million facility live 31 million people who are favorably disposed to CART by Nigel Mansell's success in the series. Peter Davis is the CEO, and Gerry Forsythe, the biggest private shareholder in CART, is a backer. Forsythe is also a substantial backer of Fundidora Park, a new two mile road course in Monterrey, Mexico, which has the privilege of starting off the 2001 CART FedEx Championship Series. Ron Dickson, the experienced Australian manager installed by Gerry has a set of financial statistics that would be the envy of many American promoters. All 60,000 grandstand seats sold out four months before the March 11 race date at an average price of $35 per day, most of them for a four day session. All 92 corporate suites sold out at $27,500 each. Dickson maintains that the level of enthusiasm for the event is the highest he's seen in his long motorsports career. Adrian Fernandez, with his own Tecate backed team, is sure to be a major focus of media attention.

Banking on CART...
Gerry Forsythe is a CART team owner, CART's largest individual shareholder, now has an interest in two major new CART circuits.

Bob Steig

DAYTONA™ FINISH LINE PERFORMANCE

Kick Some Asphalt!

UNI-T Technology + Three Great Tires = A Higher Standard Of Performance.

Strive for perfection? Us? OK, we admit it, we can't help ourselves. The same spirit that has made us a winner on the Indy Lights championship racing track is driving us to deliver the winning edge in passenger tire performance. The result of this relentless dedication to performance can be seen in the Daytona® SR, HR and ZR tires, all of which now feature the added benefits of **UNI-T**–the **U**ltimate **N**etwork of **I**ntelligent **T**ire **T**echnology!

Daytona SR with UNI-T–When you combine stylish good looks, unique tread design, and an affordable price, the result is this S- and T-rated tire. The 4- and 5-rib designs feature wide grooves to help resist hydroplaning as well as deliver great overall wet performance. With both blackwall and raised white letter sidewall styling available, the Daytona SR delivers the exact combination of looks, value and performance your customers are looking for!

Daytona HR with UNI-T–Everything your customers demand from an H-rated performance tire, at an affordable price. The directional tread design with large slots and sipes is designed to help evacuate water and provide surefooted traction and handling in a variety of conditions. Through **UNI-T** technology, the new Daytona HR outperforms the current Daytona HR/4 in both wet and dry conditions.

Daytona ZR with UNI-T–Ultra-high performance with exceptional value! The Z-rated passenger tire combines directional performance tread design with technology learned from our Dayton Daytona racing tires. The stylish mirrored sidewall complements the sweeping lines of the radically new tread pattern. Whatever the season, the ultra-high performance Daytona ZR quietly offers outstanding handling, grip and steering response.

The Daytona SR, HR and ZR are covered by the following warranties:
• 100% FREE replacement manufacturer's warranty* • 30 Day Test Drive Warranty**
• Daytona SR–55,000 mile treadwear warranty*** • Daytona HR–40,000 mile treadwear warranty***

Daytona® SR
With **UNI-T**
4-Rib

Daytona® SR
With **UNI-T**
5-Rib

Daytona® HR
With **UNI-T**

Daytona® ZR
With **UNI-T**

DAYTON®
Performance for Every Road™

www.daytontire.com

Dayton Indy Lights

New Zealander Scott Dixon Wins Six Times En Route to the Title

Winning five of the year's first 11 races in a 12 race campaign should have put a lock on the 2000 Dayton Indy Lights championship for Scott Dixon, PacWest's handsome young blond driver from New Zealand. It didn't. He crashed out of two events preceding the Fontana finale and persistent, season long pursuer rookie Townsend Bell, a Barber Dodge graduate, won at Gateway, placed second in the other, at Houston. Dorricott Racing teammate Casey Mears was the runner-up at Gateway, the winner at Houston. Dixon's 42 point bulge over Bell prior to Gateway was now down to four with Mears lurking close behind with a five point deficit. Clearly Dixon would have to regain his winning form at Fontana, or something very close to it, to take the title. He did just that, qualifying on the front row, and handily holding off Bell, who gained the runner-up honors from a lowly 16th on the starting grid, attributed to engine problems in qualifying. Dixon acknowledged his debt to PacWest teammate Tony Renna who provided an efficient drafting partnership, one that the Dorricott pair of Bell and Mears were unable to match. Renna took down third place in the race, followed by Mears. Bell garnered second place in the championship chase with third falling to Mears. Dixon will be amply rewarded for his championship effort. He has gained a seat on PacWest's Champ Car team in 2001, a rebuilding year in which the once high flying group attempts to return to winning ways.

Repeating Dorricott Racing's 1999 sweep of the Dayton Indy Lights Series' top three places would be difficult under any circumstances, virtually impossible when two of the three drivers, champion Oriol Servia and Philipp Peter were gone. But Dorricott gave it their usual intense effort.

Casey Mears, the only holdover, was the pre-season favorite for the title, but early in the actual campaign new recruit Jason Bright appeared to have the best shot at the championship. He won at Portland and actually led the points parade after Michigan. However, a severe pre-race crash at Chicago took him out of that event - and despite a pole and a courageous third place at Mid-Ohio - out of contention for top honors in the championship. He placed sixth. Bright's misfortune passed the torch to Bell and Mears who responded admirably. Bell won at Mid-Ohio and Gateway. He earned two poles and four runner-up finishes and ended the year in second place with 146 points to Dixon's 155. He plans to be back with Dorricott in 2001 and looms as the off-season favorite for the title after gaining 2000 Rookie of the Year honors.

Casey Mears, nephew of Champ Car luminary Rick Mears, had, surprisingly, never won a Dayton Indy Lights race in his four years on the circuit until Houston this year. He also won two poles and placed second three times. He collected 141 points, good for third place in the championship where he was the 1999 runner-up. Bobby Rahal gave him a nice post season present, a one-off ride in the FedEx Championship Series season finale. He responded by qualifying respectably, leading 10 laps and finishing fourth in a race marked by attrition. Despite his desire to stay in CART, his marketable name, and his favorable Fontana reviews, no place opened up for him in 2001 and he has accepted an offer in the Indy Racing Northern Light Series.

Felipe Giaffone was the leading pole producer of the year with three, earned his first Dayton Indy Lights win, a dominating drive at Michigan, plus a pair of runner-up placements. It all added up to 118 points and fourth in the year's championship. He also had a Champ Car test driver assignment this year (Mo Nunn Racing) but is unsettled on his plans for 2001. Another Barber Dodge graduate, Tony Renna, failed to match the win he scored in his 1998 rookie season but did make three podium appearances among his seven top five placements. He'll be back at PacWest in 2001, this time as the lead driver. His 105 points earned him fifth place in the year's total.

Jeff Simmons, the two-time Barber Dodge champion, made the podium three times in his rookie season with Team KOOL Green, earned points in every race except two. His 88 point total came out to seventh place for the year.

Simmons' teammate, Jonny Kane, the 1999 Rookie of the Year, had a frustrating season. A pre-season candidate for top honors in 2001, he was on the pole at the Long Beach opener but went off course and finished sixth. He got back in form with the victory in Detroit but four later DNFs cancelled any title aspirations. He scored just 52 points for the year, landing in 10th place, after fourth place in 1999, the highest rank for any driver not wearing a Dorricott badge.

Mario Dominguez, the top Mexican driver of the five in the series, didn't match his single win of 1999 but did score a podium position and 67 points for eighth place on the season ladder, followed by Chris Menninga with 61 points in ninth place.

Since virtually every driver in the series eyes a Champ Car ride as his objective, a positive note for the year is the achievement of that goal by Dixon, after only two seasons in Dayton Indy Lights, and Mears' move to the IRNL ranks, with a shot at the Indianapolis 500, won four times by Uncle Rick.

Steve Swope

Bob Steig

Dayton's Joe Barbieri can be justifiably proud of the success of drivers on the company's Daytona radials in 2000, the third year that Dayton has been the Series' exclusive tire supplier. Not only did they handle speeds in excess of 190 mph, on the superspeedways, but two in the ranks graduated to higher levels of single-seater competition. Champion Scott Dixon, in action, left, moved up to PacWest's FedEx Championship Series team and Casey Mears graduated to the Galles Racing team in the Indy Racing Northern Light Series.

New for 2001 is the Dayton Indy Lights Series' first Latin American foray, supporting the season opener in the CART FedEx Championship Series at Fundidora Park in Monterrey, Mexico, on March 11th. Enthusiasm for the four day weekend in Monterrey was high; all grandstand seats and entertainment suites were sold well ahead of race date. The outing could prove advantageous for the five Mexican drivers in the series in 2000: Mario Dominguez, Rodolfo Lavin, Rudy Junco Jr., Rolando Quintanilla and Luis Diaz. Despite the home country edge for this quintet, the pre-race favorite will be American Townsend Bell, the 2000 Rookie of the Year and the leading candidate for top honors in 2001.

Cheryl Day Anderson

1 Winner of six races, including the Fontana finale **SCOTT DIXON** scored the Dayton Indy Lights Championship and a swift elevation to the FedEx Championship Series in 2001. (155 Dayton Indy Lights points)

Cheryl Day Anderson

2 Rookie **TOWNSEND BELL**, up from the Barber Dodge ranks, won twice, notched a pair of poles, but came up just short in the championship chase. (146 Dayton Indy Lights points)

Dayton Indy Lights Race 3
Tenneco Automotive Grand Prix of Detroit
The Raceway on Belle Isle
June 18, 2000

JONNY KANE REBOUNDS IN DETROIT FOR HIS FIRST VICTORY OF 2000

The new season had not been kind to Jonny Kane. He lost the season opener to his own driving error, lost round two to an errant wheel. However, in Detroit, the luck of the Irish prevailed. Kane won the pole position, his second of the year, and led throughout, handling two restarts masterfully. Casey Mears was the second fastest qualifier but was edged on the start by Felipe Giaffone, third fastest in qualifying. They ended up in that order, Giaffone second, Mears third, as Kane ran away from the pack on both restarts, occasioned when first Jason Bright and then Tony Renna found the wall in separate single car encounters. Fourth quickest qualifier PacWest Racing's Scott Dixon, the winner on both previous outings, was unable to improve his position and settled for fourth place in the race. Team Mexico's Mario Dominguez, fastest of the five Mexican drivers in the event, was the fifth driver across the finish line. It was a big day for former Dayton Indy Lights drivers in the day's featured FedEx Championship Series event, the Tenneco Automotive Grand Prix of Detroit. Helio Castroneves was the winner (his first victory) and rookie Oriol Servia, the 1999 Dayton Indy Lights champion, gained his first podium. 1990 champion Paul Tracy and 1998 champion Cristiano da Matta as well as Lights graduates Adrian Fernandez and Luiz Garcia also competed in the event.

Cheryl Day Anderson

Dayton Indy Lights Race 4
Freightliner/G.I. Joe's 200
Portland International Raceway
June 25, 2000

JASON BRIGHT TOPS AN ALL ROOKIE PODIUM IN PORTLAND

Things were anything but bright for Australian rookie Jason Bright in his last outing - in Detroit. He crashed on the first lap. This time he out-sprinted Dorricott teammate and polesitter Townsend Bell on the first green flag lap and led all the way to the checker. Bell pressured the leader all the way but could never make the pass. Nor could Jeff Simmons, who moved up to third place from sixth on the grid, get by Bell. They finished in that order, Bright, Bell and Simmons, for an all rookie winner's podium. Bell and Simmons are Barber Dodge graduates who are figuring prominently in this year's Dayton Indy Lights campaign. PacWest's Tony Renna and Conquest Racing's Chris Menninga rounded out the top five. Team KOOL Green's Jonny Kane, winner of the previous Detroit round, and Scott Dixon, winner of the first two events, had less than stellar outings. Kane retired with engine problems. Dixon had qualifying problems, starting eighth, and ending up 11th after an early race tangle with Kane. He set the race's fastest lap trying to get back up front.

Dayton Indy Lights Race 5
Michigan 500
Michigan Speedway
July 23, 2000

FELIPE GIAFFONE GETS HIS FIRST DAYTON INDY LIGHTS WIN ON THE SUPERFAST MICHIGAN SPEEDWAY

Felipe Giaffone roared into the Dayton Indy Lights winner's column at Michigan after 39 previous tries which yielded only a quartet of runner-up finishes. From the pole, the fourth of his career, he led every lap of the first 48, when he seemingly was passed by a flying Tony Renna, the winner here in 1998. PacWest's Renna, third fastest in qualifying, had just passed Casey Mears, who had been dogging leader Giaffone all race. The race stewards had different ideas, ruling that the Renna passes were under the yellow flag, occasioned by the front wing that fell off of the car of Brian Stewart Racing's Rodolfo Lavin. The officials moved Renna back to third place as the race ended under yellow. While the results had Giaffone smiling in victory circle, Mears was understandably unhappy. He wanted a last lap shoot-out, having lost one to then teammate Philipp Peter here last year. Townsend Bell ran a strong race coming up to fourth place from way back, but not in time to aid teammate Mears in the draft. Fifth place went to Todd Snyder. Scott Dixon had another disappointing outing, finishing a lap down in 14th after a pit stop for a cut tire, likely incurred in incidents with Justin Bell and Rodolfo Lavin. Jason Bright, the ninth place finisher, set the fastest lap at 191.037 mph and took over the points lead at 57, ahead of Dixon and Mears, tied at 56.

Cheryl Day Anderson

Dayton Indy Lights Race 6
TARGET Grand Prix
Chicago Motor Speedway
July 23, 2000

SCOTT DIXON REBOUNDS IN CHICAGO FOR HIS THIRD VICTORY OF 2000

Scott Dixon had won the year's first two races but the next three had proved problematical. Round six, in Chicago, turned out to be the charm. He rebounded for a clear cut victory even though the race ended under caution when third place Casey Mears and second place Chris Menninga, the pole winner, tangled two laps from the end. They took each other out in a spectacular encounter that saw Mears' car land on top of Menninga's. Dixon himself escaped from a first lap incident that put Todd Snyder and Rolando Quintanilla on the sidelines. Townsend Bell and Tony Renna, who came up from the last row at the start, capitalized on the Mears-Menninga mix-up to finish second and third. Felipe Giaffone and Rodolfo Lavin completed the top five in an accident depleted field. Dorricott Racing's rapid rookie Jason Bright, second in the points going into Chicago, missed the race due to a practice mishap as did Jonny Kane who crashed in qualifying. His replacement, Derek Higgins, finished 13th. The only problem Dixon encountered in his runaway victory, in which he led at times by 17 seconds, was a stubborn Mario Dominguez whom he lapped three times. The win padded leader Dixon's margin in the points standings over second place Giaffone to 12. Dixon has now won half of the year's races to date. Not bad for a rookie.

Dayton Indy Lights Race 7
Miller Lite 200
Mid-Ohio Sports Car Course
August 13, 2000

TOWNSEND BELL JUMPS OUT TO HIS FIRST DAYTON INDY LIGHTS VICTORY AT MID-OHIO

Dorricott Racing teammates Townsend Bell and Jason Bright owned the front row starting positions at Mid-Ohio with pole winner Bright on the inside. However, it was Bell who scorched off the starting line at the green flag to take the lead into the first turn with Bright in determined but frustrated pursuit. That's where Bell stayed all 42 laps to the checkered flag; the first in his brief Dayton Indy Lights career. Chicago winner Scott Dixon barged through traffic from an eighth place starting slot to edge a gallant Bright, still hurting from his Chicago practice injuries, for runner-up honors. Tony Renna finished fourth, ahead of Casey Mears who set the race's fastest lap. Dixon retained his lead in the points campaign by 13 over new second place producer Bell. Bright admitted post-race that he had been snookered at the start, but thought the starter would wave it off. Mexican countrymen Luiz Diaz and Rodolfo Lavin tangled mid-race, putting both on the sidelines. A substitute in the previous event, Derek Higgins returned to the series full-time, placing seventh for the Mexpro Racing team.

Cheryl Day Anderson

Dayton Indy Lights Race 8
Molson Indy Vancouver
Concord Pacific Place
September 3, 2000

SCOTT DIXON SNATCHES THE WIN AT VANCOUVER

Alongside pole winner Felipe Giaffone on the front row at the start, Scott Dixon hounded the race leader for 35 laps. On lap 36, the pressure got to Giaffone. He made a slight error, enabling Dixon to slide by for the lead and the checkered flag. PacWest's Dixon built up a husky cushion of 7.845 seconds over runner-up Giaffone in his half dozen laps in the lead. Jeff Simmons, who started on the inside of the second row, finished the same way, occupying the third slot on the winner's podium. Fourth place Townsend Bell was repeatedly on Simmons' tailpipe but never realistically in a position to pass. Mario Dominguez did get by Tony Renna for fifth place. On the start, Chris Menninga tangled with Andy Boss, taking both of them out. Their altercation involved Jason Bright who made repairs and returned to the fray, hopelessly behind. On the lap four restart, Luis Diaz bunted Jonny Kane into the sidelines but was able to continue himself after a pit stop, albeit two laps down. With his fourth victory in eight starts, Dixon retained his .500 winning average in the series and was now a handsome 21 points ahead of second place Bell, and 30 points up on third place Giaffone.

Dayton Indy Lights Race 9
Honda Grand Prix of Monterey
Laguna Seca Raceway
September 10, 2000

SCOTT DIXON DOMINATES AT LAGUNA SECA, PADS HIS CHAMPIONSHIP LEAD

It took only three laps from the start for Scott Dixon to surge past pole winner Casey Mears on the beautiful Laguna Seca road circuit. Dixon was in total command for the remaining 31 circuits, arriving at the checker 2.885 seconds ahead of runner-up Mears, who was unable to convert his first Dayton Indy Lights pole into his first win in the series. Third fastest qualifier Jeff Simmons couldn't pressure Mears, nor could Tony Renna, fourth fastest in qualifying, pressure Simmons. They finished as they started with the third and fourth placements. Jonny Kane, already saddled with too many DNFs this year, was happy to settle for the final top five finish. Dorricott Racing's Townsend Bell was the loser in an altercation with Derek Higgins. Bell was sidelined while Higgins managed to stay on the lead lap. Later, Rodolfo Lavin and Waldemar Coronas indulged in an all-Mexican encounter which put both a lap down at the finish. With five victories in nine events, Dixon's winning average is over .500 and he is an odds-on favorite for the title with a 42 point bulge in the points chase, over Bell, with three events remaining. Bell's crash was a severe blow to his title aspirations at this late stage in the season.

Dayton Indy Lights Race 10
Motorola 300
Gateway International Raceway
September 17, 2000

TOWNSEND BELL THE WINNER AT GATEWAY AS DORRICOTT RACING SCORES A SWEEP

All three winners' podium places at Gateway went to Dorricott Racing drivers, led by Townsend Bell, scored a sweep, never before achieved by any Dayton Indy Lights team. Bell led every lap from the pole. Early challenger Scott Dixon, driving for the PacWest team, spun into the wall after 18 laps of a fruitless pursuit. Late challenger Jeff Simmons, in Team KOOL Green colors, did the same after 56 circuits. This sequence left Dorricott teammates Jason Bright and Casey Mears running second and third. They later switched places but it was still an all-Dorricott line-up on the winner's podium. Mears' accomplishment was outstanding since he started back on the fourth row. PacWest's Tony Renna nailed down fourth place and the final top five placement went to Chris Menninga. With Bell winning the extra points for the pole and fastest lap and Dixon in the DNF column, the points race tightened up. Dixon now leads by only 20 markers but can still put the title into his logbook next time out in Houston.

Dayton Indy Lights Race 11
Texaco/Havoline Grand Prix of Houston
Houston Street Course
October 1, 2000

A BIG DAY FOR CASEY MEARS AT HOUSTON, HIS FIRST DAYTON INDY LIGHTS VICTORY

Close on five occasions, Casey Mears had never scored a victory in 46 Dayton Indy Lights starts before the Houston round. On his 47th try, triumph came his way in stellar fashion. He led every lap from the pole, with a solid 1.241 second cushion over Dorricott teammate Townsend Bell at the finish. Conquest Racing's Felipe Giaffone sliced his way up to third place at the end from seventh at the start. He was aided by a crash triggered by Jonny Kane's exploding gearbox, oil from which took out Derek Higgins, and points leader Scott Dixon as well. This development reduced Dixon's points lead to a mere four over Bell and five over Mears. Dixon can now afford no missteps in the Fontana finale to nail down the title that seemed secure only two races ago. Bell and Mears, with less to lose, can afford to go all out. Lucas Motorsports' Geoff Boss finished fourth with Conquest Racing's Chris Menninga right behind in fifth place. As icing on his cake, Mears also came up with the race's fastest lap. He also got a handsome bonus, a one-off ride in a Team Rahal Champ Car at Fontana.

Dayton Indy Lights Race 12
Marlboro 500 Presented by Toyota
California Speedway
October 29, 2000

SCOTT DIXON
FLIES AT FONTANA,
TAKES THE RACE VICTORY
AND THE DAYTON
INDY LIGHTS
CHAMPIONSHIP

Pole winner Felipe Giaffone led the first lap on California's big, fast two mile oval. All the rest belonged to Scott Dixon as he snared his sixth win of the year and the Dayton Indy Lights title. Closest challenger Townsend Bell made a gallant, if unsuccessful bid. He started back in 16th place due to a malfunctioning engine in qualifying but was a mere .016 second behind Dixon at the finish. Bell easily earned Rookie of the Year honors to go on top of his second place in the championship. Dixon readily credited PacWest teammate Tony Renna, his drafting mate, with the generous assistance that made his victory possible. Renna finished third. By contrast, Dorricott Racing's Casey Mears had trouble finding a suitable drafting partner since teammate Bell was also in the hunt for the championship. Mears finished fourth, ahead of fifth place Rodolfo Lavin who led a pack consisting of Jeff Simmons, Felipe Giaffone and Rudy Junco, Jr. Genoa Racing's Cory Witherill surprised observers by posting the race's fastest lap, a sizzling 193.617 mph. With Dixon finishing the season with the .500 winning average he had maintained most of the year, it was no surprise that he was awarded a seat on PacWest's FedEx Championship Series team, rebuilding in 2001 after several lackluster years.

Winner of six races in the 2000 season, newly crowned Dayton Indy Lights Champion Scott Dixon celebrates in victory circle.

Cheryl Day Anderson

Congratulations

Nilton Rossoni
2000 Barber Dodge Pro Series
Champion

www.niltonrossoni.com

Anthony Simone
2000 Formula Dodge
National Championship
Champion

Ryan Hunter-Reay
2000 Barber Dodge Pro Series
Rookie-of-the-Year

Barber Dodge Pro Series

Nilton Rossoni Wins Six Times Nails Down the Title

Brazilian Nilton Rossoni served notice in the Watkins Glen final event of 1999 that he was the favored candidate for top honors in 2000 by leading every lap from the pole. With last year's top three, Jeff Simmons, Todd Snyder and Townsend Bell, graduated to first class Dayton Indy Lights rides in 2000, Californian Jon Fogarty, the only other proven race winner in the 2000 field, loomed as Rossoni's prime competitor. For once the prognosticators proved to be right. Rossoni posted a remarkable winning average of .500 taking top honors in six of the 12 events, including the season opener at Sebring, in support of the EXXON Superflo 12 hour race, and the finale, the first stand alone event in series history. Rossoni set new race average speed records in both. Fogarty, a tenacious opponent, gained the series runner-up honors by winning three events, Lime Rock, Detroit and Mid-Ohio, two from the pole, and setting a pair of new race records in the bargain. In another year this output might have been enough to take the title but not this time. Fogarty was 20 points in arrears of champion Rossoni at season end. Rossoni's handsome year end bonus boosted his season's prize money to $405,700. Fogarty earned $75,100. Both move up to Dayton Indy Lights in 2001; Rossoni with Conquest Racing, Fogarty with powerhouse Dorricott.

The year's only other race winners were Dutchman Sepp Koster, winner of a frigid and snow plagued Nazareth round, Matt Plumb, who prevailed in Vancouver, and Michael Valiante, the Road Atlanta victor. For all three, it was a first time trip to the top podium level and an indicator of more victories to come. Koster placed third in the championship, Plumb was the year's fourth highest in points production and Valiante's late season victory earned him sixth place. Co-Rookie of the Year in 1999, he was the surprise pole winner in his first Barber Dodge event, the year's first race, and was only dislodged from the lead by eventual winner Rossoni only after 36 of the 39 laps scheduled. Rookie Ryan Hunter-Reay of Boca Raton, entered the season as the Barber Dodge Pro Series Big Scholarship winner. He left with a top five season ranking and 2000 Rookie of the Year honors. The other 1999 Co-Rookie of the Year, Roger Yasukawa, claimed seventh place in the season's point totals, ahead of eighth place Jamie Menninga who had hoped to join big brother Chris on the roster of Barber Dodge race winners. Realization of that hope will have to wait until 2001.

Alexandre Sperafico made the podium in the season finale, earning him ninth place in the year's points totals and boding well for higher honors in 2001. Completing the year's top 10 was Sweden's Thed Björk, who didn't quite make the podium but completed a useful string of top five finishes.

Three distaff side drivers made their debuts in the Barber Dodge Pro Series in 2000, Sara Senske, Rhonda Trammell and Milka Duno, livening the proceedings, but none managed to crack the year's top 10. Senske was the top producer of the trio with 16 points for the season.

Andrew Lally, who missed three events, had a promising season start, making the podium in all three of the year's first three races, including runner-up honors at Lime Rock. The absences, however, hurt his point total and he ended up just outside the top 10. While the mid-season points battle between the two top contenders was close, Rossoni's strong finish made the difference. He won the 10th round at Laguna Seca. Fogarty was the runner-up. Rossoni was on the podium at Road Atlanta's 11th round, Fogarty a lowly 15th. Rossoni could have captured the title with a conservative top 10 finish in the Homestead finale. Instead, he "came to race" and notched the victory as well as the championship. Fogarty's fourth place in the race served only to cement his runner-up status for the year by 25 points over Sepp Koster.

Over the course of the year 43 drivers competed in the series and 31 managed to get into points paying territory. The series got a big psychological boost when "old grad" Jerry Nadeau scored his first NASCAR Winston Cup victory in that series' year end race at Atlanta.

It got an even bigger boost at year end when CART made the Barber Dodge Pro Series its "Official Entry Level Professional Series."

Richard Dole

1 Clearly in command, NILTON ROSSONI won half of the year's 12 events en route to the championship and $405,7000 in winnings for the year. He moves up to the Dayton Indy Lights Series in 2001, with the strong Conquest Racing team. (175 Barber Dodge Pro Series points)

David Trimble

2 Ardent pursuer JON FOGARTY had three victories and enjoyed a period in the points lead but was no match for Rossoni's strong close out of the season. Like Rossoni, he graduates to the Dayton Indy Lights Series in 2001 with the powerful Dorricott Racing team. (155 Barber Dodge Pro Series points)

David Trimble

3 Victory at Nazareth for **SEPP KOSTER** plus three runner-up placements earned the Swedish driver third place in the points chase. (130 Barber Dodge Pro Series points)

4 Vancouver was the site of **MATT PLUMB**'s first win. Two runner-up postings helped him to fourth place for the year. (112 Barber Dodge Pro Series points)

Richard Dole

5 Rookie of the Year, **RYAN HUNTER-REAY**, cracked the year's top five and earned his first podium at Road America. The rookie title carries a $185,000 "Scholarship" prize. (104 Barber Dodge Pro Series points)

David Trimble

6 On the pole in the season opener, **MICHAEL VALIANTE** did even better at Road Atlanta where he claimed his first victory. (97 Barber Dodge Pro Series points)

David Trimble

7 Co-Rookie of the Year in 1999, **ROGER YASUKAWA** followed up with seventh place in the series in his sophomore year. (94 Barber Dodge Pro Series points)

David Trimble

8 Victory still eluded **JAMIE MENNINGA** but he made the podium in Detroit, took the pole at Homestead. (88 Barber Dodge Pro Series points)

David Trimble

9 Top result for ALEXANDRE SPERAFICO was a podium placement at the Homestead finale. (85 Barber Dodge Pro Series points)

David Trimble

10 Consistency earned the final top 10 placement for THED BJÖRK. (83 Barber Dodge Pro Series points)

Barber Dodge Pro Series Race 1
Sebring International Raceway
March 18, 2000

NILTON ROSSONI CLAIMS TOP HONORS AT SEBRING

Nilton Rossoni bested pole winner Michael Valiante in a crowd pleasing race long duel at Sebring International Raceway. The pole winner led from a determined Rossoni for 16 of the 19 laps with the front running pair out-distancing the rest of the field. On lap 17, the pressure got to Valiante and he was cleanly passed by his pursuer who had a .806 second cushion over runner-up Valiante at the finish. Third fastest qualifier, Jon Fogarty, was all alone in his third place finish. Co-Rookie of the Year in 1999, Roger Yasukawa, started fourth, finished fourth. Alexandre Sperafico picked up the final top five posting.

Already the season is shaping up as a tussle between Rossoni and Fogarty for championship honors. Valiante displayed race winning potential and could be a factor in the title chase.

Barber Dodge Pro Series Race 2
Homestead-Miami Speedway
March 25, 2000

NILTON ROSSONI LEADS EVERY LAP EN ROUTE TO HOMESTEAD VICTORY LANE

Making it a perfect two for two for the new season Nilton Rossoni registered his second victory of the year at Homestead. The rapid Brazilian made arch rival Jon Fogarty the victim of his late race passing technique this time. Fogarty had muscled surprise pole winner Andre Nicastro out of the lead on lap three and stayed in front through lap 42. After gaining second place, Rossoni had to make up ground lost in an early race tangle which he swiftly did. Rossoni got past Fogarty on lap 43 and motored away to victory with a 1.481 second advantage over runner-up Fogarty. Nicastro faded to 16th at the finish while newcomer Andy Lally put his mark on the third podium position. Matt Plumb made his way through traffic to finish fourth from ninth at the start while Thed Björk earned the final top five placement with a workmanlike drive.

Barber Dodge Pro Series Race 3
Nazareth Speedway
April 10, 2000

SEPP KOSTER GETS HIS FIRST VICTORY IN STYLE; POLE TO POLE AT NAZARETH

Nazareth's April weather can be inhospitable, cold and rainy, but never before had it snowed on race day. The featured CART FedEx Championship Series officials postponed their round and packed up. The Dayton Indy Lights crew braved it out and ran on Monday. There was no official qualifying, but Dutchman Sepp Koster was awarded the number one starting position on the basis of practice timing. This boost was all he needed. He ran off every lap in the lead. Not that it was easy, rookie Ryan Hunter-Reay hounded him unrelentingly along the way but was forced to accept the runner-up slot a scant 0.585 second behind at the checker. Andy Lally checked into the third podium position, his second such placement in a row. Michael Valiante and Roger Yasukawa had a race long dice for the two remaining lap five places with Valiante prevailing in fourth.

Richard Dole

Barber Dodge Pro Series Race 4	Barber Dodge Pro Series Race 5	Barber Dodge Pro Series Race 6
The Dodge Dealers Grand Prix	The Raceway at Belle Isle Park	Burke Lakefront Airport
at Lime Rock Park	Detroit, MI	Cleveland, OH
May 29, 2000	June 18, 2000	July 1, 2000

JON FOGARTY DOMINATES THE DODGE DEALERS GRAND PRIX AT LIME ROCK

A BEAUTIFUL DAY ON BELLE ISLE FOR JON FOGARTY, HIS SECOND WIN IN A ROW

NILTON ROSSONI REBOUNDS TO CAPTURE TOP HONORS IN CLEVELAND

Californian Jon Fogarty ran away with Barber Dodge's Lime Rock round, leading every lap from the pole. He was more than 10 seconds ahead of runner-up Andy Lally at the finish. Fogarty arch rival, Nilton Rossoni, was off the pace for the second race in a row, earning a mere three points from his 13th place finish. Fogarty left the day's battleground with an 18 point lead in the championship chase. Peter Boss, the latest in a long line of racers from Rhode Island, had his best outing of the year claiming the third podium position. Boca Raton based rookie Ryan Hunter-Reay finished fourth, just ahead of Brazil's Alexandre Sperafico.

Setting a torrid mid-season pace, Jon Fogarty won his second wire-to-wire victory on Detroit's challenging Belle Isle street circuit. He set a new race average speed record while piling up a 3.878 second advantage over runner-up Matt Plumb. Still pursuing victory, Jamie Menninga had his best outing of the year, garnering the third podium position, after starting on the front row. Andre Nicastro and Roger Yasukawa completed the top five. Brazilian Nilton Rossoni, started in 10th, finished in sixth, losing further ground in the championship hunt to Fogarty who is setting the pace. Rossoni, the pre-season title favorite, will have to turn up the wick to catch Fogarty.

Cleveland's wide runway straights and sweeping turns offer multiple passing opportunities for drivers and lots of action for spectators. However, none of the other 25 competitors could catch pole winner Nilton Rossoni, or even come very close. He led every lap, finishing a comfortable 2.971 seconds ahead of Dutchman Sepp Koster at the checker. Jon Fogarty, the third fastest qualifier, made some daring moves to get around the front runners but could not improve on his starting position. He did retain third place in the race and his hold on the points leadership. Thed Björk snapped up the fourth finishing place ahead of Roger Yasukawa in fifth.

Barber Dodge Pro Series Race 7
Mid-Ohio Sports Car Course
August 13, 2000

JON FOGARTY MASTERS MID-OHIO FOR HIS THIRD WIN OF THE YEAR

Swedish rookie Thed Björk was the sensation of the Mid-Ohio weekend. He qualified on the pole and led all the way until his oil pressure dropped precipitously on a lap 19 restart. Second fastest qualifier Jon Fogarty and the rest of the leading pack swooped past him, dropping the unfortunate Swede right out of the top 10. Winner Fogarty had a clear .943 second edge over championship rival Nilton Rossoni, the runner-up, at the finish. Sepp Koster, the third driver figuring prominently in the championship chase, notched third place in the race to stay in the hunt. Jamie Menninga and Andy Lally rounded out the top five. Fogarty's win bolstered his lead in the championship chase going past the halfway mark with Rossoni ardently chasing the front runner.

Barber Dodge Pro Series Race 8
Road America
August 20, 2000

NILTON ROSSONI ROLLS TO ROAD AMERICA VICTORY

Nilton Rossoni loves fast road courses, which means that Road America's daunting four mile layout was the ideal setting for his fourth victory of the year. In the process he won the pole, set a record race lap and a new record average for the race. Also helping his championship bid was a lackluster performance by rival Jon Fogarty. Fogarty finished ninth, giving Rossoni a 14 point advantage in the day's point production with the season heading into its final third. Jamie Menninga survived an encounter with Matt Plumb to finish second. Plumb was sidelined. Rapid rookie Ryan Hunter-Reay notched his second podium finish of the year. Roger Yasukawa finished fourth, ahead of championship contender Sepp Koster, the last driver in the top five.

Barber Dodge Pro Series Race 9
Vancouver Street Circuit
September 2, 2000

MATT PLUMB VICTORIOUS IN VANCOUVER

Matt Plumb made the street course in beautiful downtown Vancouver the scene of his first Barber Dodge Pro Series victory. Plumb was the third fastest qualifier behind a pair of rookies. Second fastest Andy Lally tried to pass pole-sitter Ryan Hunter-Reay on lap two and failed, with disastrous results for both. The encounter left Lally on the sidelines and Hunter-Reay out of contention and an eighth place finish to show for his sparkling qualifying effort. Plumb played a cooler hand than the rookies and made no mistakes on his way to victory number one. Sepp Koster gained some momentum in his championship challenge with runner-up honors while the points leaders Jon Fogarty and Nilton Rossoni took down fifth and fourth places. Andre Nicastro finished third.

Richard Dole

Barber Dodge Pro Series Race 10
Laguna Seca Raceway
September 10, 2000

NILTON ROSSONI SURVIVES A BUMPING ENCOUNTER TO SNARE LAGUNA SECA VICTORY

Nilton Rossoni took the Laguna Seca pole as the first step in one of his trademark wire-to-wire victories. Matt Plumb, flush from his Vancouver triumph, spoiled that game plan. Alongside Rossoni on the front row he promptly took the lead away from the Brazilian and held it for the first five laps. Rossoni then executed a daring pass on the notorious corkscrew corner that dislodged Plumb from the lead and sent him spinning into the desert. Nobody else came close, but arch rival Jon Fogarty claimed second place and retained a tenuous six point lead in the championship hunt. Andy Lally posted another podium placement as Alexandre Sperafico and Ryan Hunter-Reay completed the top five. Sepp Koster attracted the fans attention with a daring drive from 18th on the starting grid to third before mechanical failure ended his run on the last lap. With Rossoni and Fogarty so close in the championship chase, the title will hinge on the year's last two events, Road Atlanta and Homestead. While Fogarty leads, Rossoni's victory here puts momentum on his side. Sepp Koster, Matt Plumb and Jamie Menninga failed to score any points today. Koster dropped out with mechanical problems. Plumb and Menninga were contact victims after only five laps. Before his mechanical misfortune, Koster had the fans cheering with a dashing drive from 18th on the grid to the heels of the leading pack. With a little more luck he could be a multiple race winner this year.

Rossoni has gained maturity along with his speed and is looking more and more like a solid candidate for a Dayton Indy Lights ride in 2001.

Barber Dodge Pro Series Race 11
Road Atlanta
September 30, 2000

LUCK TURNS FOR MICHAEL VALIANTE. HE ROARS TO ROAD ATLANTA VICTORY

Fate had not been kind to Michael Valiante in his debut Barber Dodge season. He had demonstrated both speed and talent but had little in the way of solid results to show for his efforts. On the challenging Road Atlanta circuit it all came together for the Canadian rookie. Pole position at a new record speed, every lap in the lead, victory, at a new record average speed, added up to the maximum 21 points. Along the way he set the fastest race lap. Matt Plumb, the runner-up, was the best of the rest. Title contender Nilton Rossoni settled for a solid third place that paid 14 points. Meanwhile, chief rival Jon Fogarty had mega-sized misfortune. He tangled with another car at the start, crippling his car's aerodynamics and finished a lowly 15th, good for only a single point. This left Rossoni in the admirable position of needing only a safe top 10 finish in the finale to capture the title. Jamie Menninga and Roger Yasukawa rounded out the top five. Sara Senske almost made the top 10, finishing 11th. Thed Björk, again displayed talent but had only sixth place to show for his efforts. When Rossoni and Fogarty go head-to-head for the title in the season's finale at Homestead, the pressure will be on Fogarty. If Rossoni elects a conservative game plan, Fogarty's best efforts may go for naught. Valiante has now become a race winner, in virtuoso fashion. When this item is added to his proven skills as a qualifier, he becomes a leading candidate for next year's championship with a year's experience in his logbook. Valiante's speed, coupled with another year's seasoning in Barber Dodge, should make him eligible for graduation to Dayton Indy Lights.

Barber Dodge Pro Series Race 12
Homestead-Miami Speedway
October 8, 2000

ROSSONI CAPTURES THE RACING FOR KIDS GRAND PRIX - AND THE BARBER DODGE PRO SERIES CHAMPIONSHIP

A stylish Nilton Rossoni could have cruised to the Barber Dodge Pro Series Championship and its big $300,000 year end bonus. All he needed in the Homestead finale, the first ever stand alone Barber Dodge Pro race, was a top 10 finish. Instead, he elected to go all out and register his sixth win of the year. Starting fourth, he got by pole winner Jamie Menninga on lap seven. A flying Sepp Koster displaced him from the point for a single lap by posting the race's fastest lap. Rossoni immediately repassed and stayed in command the rest of the way. At the end, he owned a 2.243 second cushion over Koster in the race and a 20 point final advantage over Jon Fogarty in the championship. Fogarty's fourth place today left him solidly in second place in the championship over Koster. Alex Sperafico notched the race's last podium position, with fifth going to Matt Plumb. Plumb also earned fourth place in the championship chase. Today's seventh place runner, Ryan Hunter-Reay, notched fifth place in the points and Rookie of the Year honors and a $185,000 "Scholarship" prize.

In a highly competitive season, qualifying and race records fell to new marks in abundance, and the top two drivers, Rossoni and Fogarty, like their predecessors, earned berths with top drawer Indy Lights teams; Conquest for Rossoni, Dorricott for Fogarty. In the pre-season ratings for 2001 honors Plumb is given the edge on experience with Valiante and Hunter-Reay close behind. With CART's announcement of the Barber Dodge Pros Series as its "official" entry level professional series, Barber Dodge takes on a new dimension.

Steve Swope

NASCAR Winston Cup Series

Bobby Labonte Learns Patience, Takes the Winston Cup

Patience, patience, that's all it took for Bobby Labonte to deliver the Winston Cup that he promised team owner Joe Gibbs when he came aboard in 1995. He had all the other ingredients, his own well-honed driving skills, a superb team headed by crew chief Jimmy Makar and engine builder Mark Cronquist, and, in Gibbs, an inspirational owner with deep pockets. But the 36 year old veteran had that same platform last year when he had to settle for second place on the grueling Winston Cup circuit. This year he concentrated on finishing, and finish he did. Not a single DNF blotted his record or marred his point total. Even though his four victories of 2000 didn't match his five wins of 1999, the likeable Labonte posted 19 top five finishes, four more than any other driver and 24 top 10 placements, a feat matched only by 2000 runner-up Dale Earnhardt and 1999 champion Dale Jarrett, the fourth place campaigner this year. Even before the 2000 season started, Jarrett had named Labonte as the man he had to beat for a second title in a row.

Not exactly a stranger to the Winston Cup awards, he was on brother Terry's winning team in 1984 at the entry level, Bobby moved smoothly through his starring role in a week of frenetic activity in New York. Monday, a helicopter tour of the city, a Tuesday luncheon at '21,' Wednesday, striking the opening bell at the New York Stock Exchange, a photo shoot in Times Square on Thursday complete with the Interstate Batteries Pontiac, a baker's dozen of television talk show appearances and, finally, the awards banquet itself on Friday, with a sellout Waldorf-Astoria audience of 1500 plus. Among the host of Fortune 500 executives on hand were Pontiac Division Manager Lynn Myers, the highest ranking female leader in the automotive industry, Andy Schindler, CEO of R.J. Reynolds, and Goodyear's top man Sam Gibara.

This carefully choreographed for live television black-tie affair is the real payoff for the Winston Cup winner. Labonte, the only brother of a previous winner to take top honors, accepted the cup - and the $3,386,640 R.J. Reynolds bonus check that came with it, from RJR Chairman Andy Schindler with the modesty that has become the hallmark of recent Cup champions.

Goodyear's Gibara added a gold plated replica of Labonte's no. 18 Pontiac, with Betty Jane France presenting NASCAR's championship ring for Bobby and diamond pendant for wife Donna on behalf of husband Bill, who was in the audience despite a strenuous regime of cancer treatments. In acceptance, Labonte displayed a crowd winning combination of assurance and humility, noting that father Bob got him started, brother Terry got him a job (admittedly involving a broom) on his championship Winston Cup team and both coached and encouraged him in his upwardly mobile driving career. Labonte has paid his dues. His record shows 10th, 11th, seventh, sixth, and his 1999 runner-up placement in the Winston Cup series after an earlier Busch Grand National championship. As a measure of Gibbs' generosity, all 125 members of his racing organization were on hand at the Waldorf to cheer Labonte on. As a measure of NASCAR's growth, Labonte's regular season's winnings of $4 million put his 2000 total at more than $7 million. Brother Terry's total take in each of his Winston Cup title years was a mere $2 million. No wonder Bobby found his New York Stock Exchange visit the most impressive experience of his big week in the Big Apple. That's where the money is and the place money can turn into wealth. If not previously, Bobby is certainly now a desireable customer for one of the blue chip Wall Street investment advisory firms.

Although Dale Jarrett started out the 2000 campaign with a second Daytona 500 victory, and Mark Martin topped the point standings for several weeks, Labonte was the clear leader over most of the strenuous campaign, needing only to fend off a challenge from a rejuvenated Dale Earnhardt to close in on the Cup. This challenge fell short. A finely focused Labonte finished a strong fourth in the penultimate Homestead round, when he could just as easily have backed into the title there. As crew chief Makar put it, "We came to race." and the Winston

2000 NASCAR Winston Cup Champion Bobby Labonte

Cup was Bobby's before the season ending Atlanta race, which turned out to be rain plagued and had to be postponed.

While Dale Earnhardt's run at an eighth championship failed, he had about as good a year as a driver can have without taking home the Cup. Prior to the start of the season some detractors felt the "Ol' Intimidator" was merely old and no longer intimidating. He confounded the naysayers by winning two races and closing out the year in second place in the Winston Cup points, good for a $2,103,995 R.J. Reynolds bonus delivered by Sports Marketing Enterprises President Rich Saunders at the Waldorf. One of Earnhardt's victories was a thrilling outing at Talladega - one of the "restrictor plate" tracks Earnhardt claims to dislike. What he does like is its contribution to the $3,701,391 in regular season prize money he earned, a $1 million Winston bonus on top of the winner's share of the race loot. Earnhardt admitted it was "tough" trying to catch up with Labonte but sent a clear warning that he was out again for his eighth title in 2001. He also admitted that 2000 "wasn't too bad a year." Indeed it wasn't. with his handsome monetary rewards - and the satisfaction of seeing from the cockpit his rookie son Dale Jr. win twice in the Earnhardt family's Budweiser backed Chevrolet.

Third place Jeff Burton, Roush Racing's top finisher in the Exide Ford moved up in the season's standings despite two less victories than his six of 1999. He noted post-season "How amazing it is that Winston helps us make so much money for something we love so much and might do for nothing." Not for nothing did Burton labor. His Winston bonus of $1,770,685 coming on top of regular season earnings of $5,121,354, made him one of the year's most highly compensated drivers. He is a leading candidate for top honors in 2001, a goal that has eluded the Roush group and its large stable of competitive drivers.

1999 Winston Cup winner Dale Jarrett, the very model of a NASCAR champion started the 2000 season in better form than his title year, with a resounding victory in the Daytona 500, NASCAR's highly burnished crown jewel and season opener. His stay at the top was short lived. He scored only one additional win late in the year, as opposed to a total of four in 1999. Consistency, the basis of his successful year earlier title run in the Ford Quality Care Taurus certainly wasn't lacking. His 15 top fives were second only to Labonte's 19 and his 24 top 10s matched the new champion's. Essentially, Labonte beat him at his own game. One item in which Labonte didn't beat him was regular season winnings of $5,225,499, the year's best. Nor was Jarrett's 2000 bonus of $1,617,376 anything to sniff at. Don't count him out in 2001.

Ricky Rudd gave up his cherished owner-driver status in 2000 to join the high-powered Robert Yates team aboard the Texaco Taurus. He also gave up the inevitable headaches that go with the dual roles. The new freedom didn't get him started on a new winning streak but it did vault him into the top five, a substantial improvement over his placement of recent years. As he said after picking up his $519,066 bonus check at the Waldorf, I've been down that road (owner-driver) and it's not worth it. He didn't even seem to mind the usual prize money split with car owner Yates.

How can you win six races, the most of any driver in 2000, twice as many as you did in 1999, and still slide back two places to sixth in the year's standings? Easy if your name is Tony Stewart and you are consumed by a diamond hard desire to win. The 1999 rookie of the year was even faster in 2000 in the Home Depot Pontiac with further development of his all out style and better track knowledge. That style sometimes overlooked the generous points rewards for lesser finishes in the scoring system. Post-season Stewart evaluated his sophomore year. "I've learned a lot this year, on and off the track." He further judged Bobby Labonte, with whom he had tangled in 1999, "the best teammate anyone could possibly have." Stewart had regular season earnings of $3,200,191 and collected an R.J. Reynolds bonus of $440,757. Team owner Gibbs, whom Stewart also praised, had the highest average season finish for his two car operation.

Rusty Wallace, in the Miller Ford, racked up a notable milestone in 2000, his 50th Winston Cup victory, one of four during the season. It wasn't the one he wanted. That, of course, is a second Cup itself. He last won top honors in 1989 and he's been banging at the door ever since. Wallace's seventh place in 2000 was his 14th in NASCAR's top 10.

Mark Martin, driver of the Valvoline Ford, is arguably NASCAR's no.1 physical fitness devotee. Despite his rigorous training regime, he took longer than expected to recover from off-season back surgery. Added to this setback, the loss of his father contributed to an eighth place result for the best driver never to have won a Winston Cup. In 13 seasons as a top flight Roush Racing pilot he's never been out of the top 10. With his remarkable physical gifts and reaction times packed into a jockey-sized

THE FASTEST QUALIFIERS 2000 WINSTON CUP POLE WINNERS	
RUSTY WALLACE	9
JEREMY MAYFIELD	4
JEFF GORDON	3
DALE JARRETT	3
BOBBY LABONTE	3
DALE EARNHARDT JR.	2
STEVE PARK	2
RICKY RUDD	2
TONY STEWART	2
JEFF BURTON	1
BILL ELLIOTT	1
TERRY LABONTE	1
MIKE SKINNER	1

frame, he could have been a successful Formula One pilot had he chosen that route early in his career. His 2000 R.J. Reynolds bonus, $334,138, came on top of regular season earnings of $3,037,721, bolstered by one victory.

For Jeff Gordon the loss of stellar crew chief Ray Evernham, his partner in three Winston Cup titles, late in 1999 didn't fully set in until the 2000 season. Gordon had lost none of his spectacular skills but the new team simply couldn't match the Gordon-Evernham chemistry. Victories slipped to three from a league leading seven in 1999 and poles were off from the previous year's eight. The net result, eighth place in the season's stand-

Times Square was one of the many choice pieces of New York real estate to fall to BOBBY LABONTE in his Pontiac-mounted invasion of the Big Apple. Bobby deemed Wall Street's New York Stock Exchange, where he rang the opening bell, as the most interesting, and the one he'd most like to have a piece of. With $7,386,640 in 2000 prize money and R.J. Reynolds' bonus award, some Wall Street firms would like a piece of his account.

ings, the lowest for Gordon since 1994. He's now a part owner of the Hendrick team and the owner of a long term driving contract with DuPont sponsorship for his Chevrolet to match. Gordon racked up Winston Cup victory no. 50 during the year, his

by winning twice and running up front regularly and with confidence. This time the title and a $50,000 check from Raybestos Brakes' Kevin Judge went to Kenseth. Though Kenseth considered himself lucky to be the newest driver in the Jack Roush sta-

Mike Helton, NASCAR's new President

Nigel Kinrade

eighth as a full time pilot, along with $292,458 RJR bonus money and $2,703,586 regular season earnings. Look for more wins and a serious run at the Cup as the new team stabilizes in 2001.

Ward Burton, along with Jeff, were again in 2000 the only pair of brothers to make NASCAR's top 10. He drove Bill Davis' Caterpillar Pontiac to a single victory in 2000, his first since 1994. His RJR bonus of $260,888 came on top of a regular season total of $2,385,326. He was the third Pontiac driver to make the year's top 10.

Among the rest of the top 20, Steve Park, who just missed the year's top 10 scored a breakthrough first Winston Cup victory as did Jerry Nadeau who just made the top 20. A fast but inconsistent Jeremy Mayfield, Rusty Wallace's teammate, had two victories but landed outside the top 20. The most intriguing rookie battle in a decade pitted Dale Earnhardt Jr., the two-time Busch Series champion, against friend and heated rival Matt Kenseth, twice his runner-up. Earnhardt Jr., driving his father's Budweiser Chevrolet, proved he had more than a name going for himself

ble, he proved himself to be quick, consistent and a worthy member of a front row group. He ended up 14th in the year's standings with $2,150,764 in earnings, two slots ahead of Earnhardt Jr., 16th on the list, and the winner of $2,610,396. Earnhardt Jr. endeared himself to the fans by his willingness and ability to dice with his "Ironhead" father and car owner for position late in races when dad was very much in contention for the Cup and every finishing slot counts mightily. A warm personality, coupled with his inherent talent, is likely to take Dale Jr. a long way. No longer need anyone ask, "Where's the next Dale Earnhardt coming from?" He's here and the original is still very much alive. The hotly contested NASCAR Manufacturers' Championship went to Ford for the second year in a row with 234 points over Pontiac with 213 and Chevrolet with 199. Edsel Ford, grandson of founder Henry, accepted the trophy and noted that among the 68 drivers contributing to Ford's 500 NASCAR wins were Richard Petty and Dale Earnhardt, stars now associated with rival makers. 2001 will mark Ford's 100th anniversary in racing.

SEASON HIGHLIGHTS

The biggest news of the year took place off the track at season's end. Highly respected NASCAR veteran Mike Helton was named president of the sanctioning body and a director as well. This move ensures that NASCAR's racing business will be managed in an evenhanded professional manner in a period of continuing expansion. Pre-season favorite Bobby Labonte never bobbled in his relentless pursuit of the Cup. Dale Earnhardt's renaissance took him almost to the top. He even out-dueled champion to be Labonte in an incredible Winston 500 at Talladega. Dodge's 2001 entry into the Winston Cup arena sprouted four new teams including Petty Enterprises alongside pointman Ray Evernham. Their debut at Daytona will be anxiously awaited. 1999 champion Dale Jarrett started the year brilliantly with a third Winston Cup win but had to wait until October to post another one. The most intriguing Rookie of the Year contest, that between Dale Earnhardt Jr. and Matt Kenseth was decided in favor of the latter, despite Earnhardt Jr.'s two to one advantage in victories. He was the first driver to score two victories in the year, not bad for a rookie. His dicing with car owner/father Dale captivated the fans. Tony Stewart's league leading six victories weren't enough to make him a serious Cup contender, but watch out next year. New $40 million annual TV contracts with Fox and NBC set monetary records but didn't sit well with incumbents CBS and ESPN. NASCAR scheduled 36 races for 2001, up from 34, meaning the campaign will get even more strenuous.

NASCAR 2000 MANUFACTURERS' CHAMPIONSHIP		
MANUFACTURER	**POINTS**	**WINS**
FORD	234	14
PONTIAC	213	11
CHEVROLET	199	9

Auto Stock

Edsel Ford accepted NASCAR's Manufacturers' Championship trophy, the company's third in the past four years, at the year end Awards dinner, an accomplishment for which he thanked Dale Jarrett, Ricky Rudd, Rusty Wallace, Mark Martin and Jeff Burton. The great grandson of the company's founder, he noted that 2001 will be the 100th anniversary of Ford Racing. In the latter half of the century, he added, 68 drivers notched more than 500 NASCAR victories in Ford cars, Galaxie, Torino, Thunderbird, Taurus and even Mercurys like Cougar and Cyclone. On the drivers' list are some of the most illustrious names in NASCAR history: Ned Jarrett, David Pearson, Freddy Lorenzen, Junior Johnson, Fireball Roberts, Bobby and Davey Allison, Alan Kulwicki, Cale Yarborough, Mario Andretti, A. J. Foyt, Richard Petty and Dale Earnhardt. He didn't forget 1988 champion Bill Elliott who was singled out for special attention, despite decamping the Ford ranks for a Dodge ride in 2001. Elliott compiled 40 NASCAR wins in Ford vehicles.

Edsel Ford, right, member of the Board, Ford Motor Company, accepts the trophy from George Pyne, NASCAR's Vice President of Marketing. Five winning Taurus drivers shown below and on adjoining page.

Nigel Kinrade

Nigel Kinrade

Some Major Players in Ford's Five Decades of NASCAR Victories

1956, Fireball Roberts, Ford Fairlane

1964, Ned Jarrett, Ford Galaxie

1965, Junior Johnson, Ford Galaxie

1965, Fred Lorenzen, Ford Galaxie

1967, Mario Andretti, Ford Galaxie

1968, Cale Yarborough, Mercury

All photos: Daytona Racing Archives

1969, LeeRoy Yarborough, Ford Torino

1969, Richard Petty, Ford Torino

1972, A.J. Foyt,
Mercury Cyclone Special

1976, David Pearson, Mercury Cougar

1978, Bobby Allison, Ford Thunderbird

1983, Dale Earnhardt, Ford Thunderbird

1985, Bill Elliott, Ford Thunderbird

1992, Alan Kulwicki, Ford Thunderbird

Nigel Kinrade

1 Propelled by Pontiac and his new found consistency, **BOBBY LABONTE** led the Winston Cup standings virtually all year and closed on the title with one race to go. Not a single DNF marred his four victory campaign. (5130 NASCAR Winston Cup points)

Nigel Kinrade

2 A rejuvenated **DALE EARNHARDT** had the best year any driver could have short of a title. His Winston 500 victory at Talladega, one of two in 2000, over champion to be Labonte was the feature of the year's most exciting race. (4865 NASCAR Winston Cup points)

3 **JEFF BURTON** matched champion Labonte in the victory column with four, but not in the all important top five and top 10 category. (4836 NASCAR Winston Cup points)

Nigel Kinrade

Nigel Kinrade

4 1999 Champion **DALE JARRETT** was again highly consistent but could only register two wins compared to four last year. (4684 NASCAR Winston Cup points)

Nigel Kinrade

5 **RICKY RUDD** moved way up the charts with his switch to the Robert Yates team from owner/driver status. Only sheer bad luck prevented him from getting back into the win column. (4575 NASCAR Winston Cup points)

6 Sophomore speedster **TONY STEWART** led the league in victories with six. If some of teammate Labonte's consistency rubs off on him in 2001 he'll be hard to beat. (4570 NASCAR Winston Cup points)

Nigel Kinrade

7 Tied for second place in 2000 victories with four **RUSTY WALLACE** was again a top qualifier but only managed to move up a single place in the year's standings. (4544 NASCAR Winston Cup points)

8 MARK MARTIN was off his 1999 pace with only a single victory and slipped five places in the year's points chart. (4410 NASCAR Winston Cup points)

Nigel Kinrade

9 In his first full year with a new crew chief **JEFF GORDON** managed three victories but the chemistry of the Evernham years was missing. (4361 NASCAR Winston Cup points)

Nigel Kinrade

10 **WARD BURTON** collected his long awaited first Winston Cup victory and made the year's top 10 for the second year in a row. (4152 NASCAR Winston Cup points)

Nigel Kinrade

11 **STEVE PARK** racked up his first victory, delighting car owner Dale Earnhardt who now has a pair of winners in his stable. He just missed the year's top 10. (3934 NASCAR Winston Cup points)

Nigel Kinrade

12 **MIKE SKINNER** again proved that he was a front runner, again came up short in his quest for an elusive first victory. (3898 NASCAR Winston Cup points)

Nigel Kinrade

Nigel Kinrade

13 JOHNNY BENSON was deprived of his first win by bad luck and the fickleness of the draft. (3716 NASCAR Winston Cup points)

15 JOE NEMECHEK was often up front and vastly improved his point standing despite not scoring a victory as he did in 1999. (3534 NASCAR Winston Cup points)

Nigel Kinrade

14 Rookie of the Year MATT KENSETH bested arch-rival and off-track friend Dale Earnhardt Jr. for 2000 honors, nailing down his first win along the way. (3716 NASCAR Winston Cup points)

16 No rookie of the year honors, but DALE EARNHARDT JR. was the first driver to score two victories in 2000, gratifying car owner and father Dale with whom he regularly diced on the track. (3516 NASCAR Winston Cup points)

17 Another disappointing year for two-time Winston Cup champion **TERRY LABONTE**, his first since 1993 without a win. (3433 NASCAR Winston Cup points)

18 A sixth straight year in the top 20 for **KEN SCHRADER** who last won in 1991. (3398 NASCAR Winston Cup points)

19 **STERLING MARLIN**'s mid-1990's magic on the superspeedways has not yet returned but he again made the year's top 20. (3363 NASCAR Winston Cup points)

20 For first time winner **JERRY NADEAU**, a breakthrough year with a front rank team, and an indication of more victories to come. (3273 NASCAR Winston Cup points)

Dale Jarrett, in the Quality Care/Ford Credit Ford, won the Daytona 500, again

DALE JARRETT DOES IT AGAIN, WINS THE DAYTONA 500

Winning the Daytona 500 once is tough enough. Winning NASCAR's premier event three times in a decade is a monumental accomplishment. Dale Jarrett did it this time with a little help from fellow Ford driver Jeff Burton. Burton's draft was the edge that propelled him past Johnny Benson, the surprise late race leader on the restart, following a caution flag with seven laps to go. Benson got his lead by taking on only two new tires on his last stop, as opposed to the standard four. So swift can fortunes change in draft dominated restrictor plate races that Benson got shuffled all the way back to 12th at the finish. For his help to Jarrett, Burton was rewarded with second place but had no opportunity for a last lap shoot-out victory when another yellow flew with two laps to go as a result of Jimmy Spencer's trip into the wall. Jarrett was the beneficiary of an uncontested first place finish. Jarrett led the most laps, 89.

Fellow Ford driver Mark Martin, the fifth place finisher, was in front for 63 laps despite an early stop for a blistered tire. Ironically, he allowed postrace that he thought he had a deal with Jarrett for the key draft. Benson, still anxiously looking for his first victory, was on top for 39 circuits and surely would have been a strong factor in the finishing flurry had it not been for the unlucky yellow. Third place starter Bill Elliott finished in the same slot. Rusty Wallace, who started on the front row, completed a Ford sweep of the first five places. Sixth place Bobby Labonte, in the Interstate Pontiac, was the first non-Ford runner, Terry Labonte was the top performer in Chevrolet's new Monte Carlo, finishing seventh. Labonte teammate Jeff Gordon, the 1999 winner, and his new team had a dismal day, finishing 34th on the basis of a failed oil line. Pre-season favorite Bobby Labonte in might have done better except for a stop-and-go penalty for a pit violation. Teammate Tony Stewart, in the Home Depot Pontiac, fared even worse, hitting a crew member on a pit stop hard enough to break his leg. If the 2000 Daytona 500 failed to set any new highs for excitement, it did set a monetary record, $2.27 million to winner Jarrett, including a $1 million Winston bonus.

BOBBY LABONTE FENDS OFF DALE EARNHARDT FOR ROCKINGHAM WIN

Pre-season title favorite Bobby Labonte lived up to his billing by holding off Dale Earnhardt to take the Dura Lube/Kmart 400 by 1.068 seconds in the race. Pontiac-mounted Labonte started third, took the lead from another Pontiac pilot, Ward Burton, on lap 281, and stayed in front for the 113 circuits remaining. Earnhardt, the fourth place starter, had the fastest car on the track at the end but couldn't overcome the handsome cushion built up by Labonte. Burton held on for third place followed by Tony Stewart and Daytona 500 winner Dale Jarrett in the top Ford. Polesitter Rusty Wallace faded to 11th on a track that chews up tires and seems to demand constant adjustment on pit stops. Labonte's win confirmed his status as best bet for the 2000 title but left him concerned that the victory might lead NASCAR officials to subtract downforce from the Pontiacs by an adjustment to the front spoiler.

DuPont Chevrolet in 2000.

Gordon had to fight off a snarling pack of fellow Chevrolet drivers in the final stages, Mike Skinner, Dale Earnhardt, and Kenny Irwin, who fin-

THE NAPA 500

Jeremy Mayfield bounced back from a disappointing Talladega experience to win his next outing

the DeWalt Tools Ford, followed by Ricky Rudd and Jeff Burton. Polesitter Mike Skinner salvaged a seventh place finish. Mayfield was the 10th different winner in the 10 events to date.

NASCAR Winston Cup Race 11
Pontiac Excitement 400
Richmond International Speedway
May 6, 2000

RICHMOND FALLS TO DALE EARNHARDT JR., HIS SECOND VICTORY OF 2000

Somebody had to do it, but nobody expected it to be a rookie. Dale Earnhardt Jr., in the Budweiser Chevrolet, became the first two race winner of the year at Richmond, adding a short track victory to his Texas Superspeedway score. He even passed his father and car owner on the last restart to take the lead. Over the last 10 laps he was under extreme pressure from Terry Labonte, a two-time winner here. Labonte couldn't find a route to a clean pass and resisted the temptation to tap young Earnhardt's bumper, settling for second place. Tony Stewart, in the Home Depot Pontiac, would have been a factor in the final countdown, except for being clipped exiting the pits by Dale Jr. and incurring a cut tire. Dale Jr. said, "I felt bad about what happened to Tony but he didn't give me a lot of room." Stewart accepted the bad break philosophically. "It wasn't his fault. It wasn't my fault, just part of racing." Ricky Rudd, in the Texaco-Havoline Ford took fourth place ahead of polesitter Rusty Wallace. Some of the points leaders had forgettable outings. Bobby Labonte and his Interstate Pontiac suffered first a spin, later a collision not of his making. Mark Martin tagged the wall when a tire went down and Jeff Burton managed only seventh place.

After the first 11 events the Winston Cup points leaders were: Bobby Labonte, 1601; Ward Burton, 1598; Mark Martin, 1568; Jeff Burton, 1542 and Dale Earnhardt, 1523.

NASCAR Winston Cup Race 12
Coca-Cola 600
Lowe's Motor Speedway
May 28, 2000

MATT KENSETH UPSTAGES FELLOW ROOKIE DALE EARNHARDT JR. TO WIN THE COCA-COLA 600

Dale Earnhardt Jr. and the Budweiser Chevrolet had the pole and the dominating roles in the 41st Coca-Cola 600, racking up 175 lead laps. Unfortunately, the last lap went to arch rival and fellow rookie Matt Kenseth in the DeWalt Tools Ford. What would have been Earnhardt Jr.'s third win of the year became Kenseth's first and propelled the Roush Racing driver into the lead for Rookie of the Year honors. Bobby Labonte and father Dale also got past Earnhardt Jr. in the closing stages to relegate him to fourth place at the finish. Dale Jarrett completed the list of top five finishers. Earnhardt Jr. still had the final laugh at the payoff window. He became the only rookie ever to win the Winston, the 70 lap big money non-points race for a select 20 drivers. He pocketed $515,000 for his brilliant run in the 10 lap final segment, beating Dale Jarrett and father Dale to the finish.

Nigel Kinrade

Matt Kenseth takes the Coca-Cola 600

Nigel Kinrade

NASCAR Winston Cup Race 13
MBNA Platinum 400
Dover Downs International Speedway
June 4, 2000

TONY STEWART SCORES IN HIS FIRST VICTORY OF 2000 AT DOVER

It took a while but no driver as fast and focused as Tony Stewart can be shut out of victory circle forever. It may have seemed like forever to Stewart, not noted for his patience, when he went winless for the first third of the new season after a sparkling rookie debut in 1999 which netted three wins and fourth place in the points along with more than $3 million in prize money. Stewart breezed home 1.215 seconds ahead of Matt Kenseth who was bidding for his sec-

ond victory in a row. Continuing to pile up points, Bobby Labonte picked up third place ahead of Dale Jarrett and his teammate Ricky Rudd. Only the top five completed all 400 laps.

NASCAR Winston Cup Race 14
Kmart 400
Michigan Speedway
June 11, 2000

NO SOPHOMORE SLUMP FOR TONY STEWART. HE TAKES KMART 400 FOR TWO IN A ROW

Leader Tony Stewart, in the Home Depot Pontiac, had a hungry trio of Dale Earnhardt, pole winner Bobby Labonte and Dale Jarrett nip-

ping at his bumper with eight laps to go when a Kenny Irwin-Geoffrey Bodine incident brought out the yellow flag. What promised to be an interesting shoot-out never happened. What did happen was rain, heavy rain and a finish under caution. An earlier downfall had delayed the proceedings by an hour and a half but the vast majority of the 130,000 spectators stuck it out to the anticlimactic final curtain. Robert Pressley, in the Jasper Engines Ford, was leading when the race was first halted and gave up the lead to Stewart on lap 185 when it was resumed. Earnhardt's competitiveness this year along with his son's is testimony to the fact that the 2000 Chevrolet Monte Carlo is improved over the 1999 model. The Sr. Earnhardt still lags leader Bobby Labonte in the points chase but is his closest pursuer.

NASCAR Winston Cup Race 15
Pocono 500
Pocono Raceway
June 17, 2000

JEREMY MAYFIELD MASTERS POCONO FOR SECOND WIN OF THE YEAR

There was no post-race jumping on the roof and no NASCAR inspection problems when Jeremy Mayfield notched his second victory of the year in the rain-delayed Pocono 500. There wasn't even a problem with Dale Earnhardt who was nudged out of the way on the final lap and ended up fourth. Earnhardt accepted his misfortune with the good grace he expects of nudged competitors when he does the nudging. Ricky Rudd claimed third place in the Texaco Ford and Mark Martin managed the fifth finishing slot. An exuberant Mayfield joined Dale Earnhardt Jr. and Tony Stewart as the year's only two-time winners. He was particularly relieved that no NASCAR inspectors dampened his celebration as was the case in his previous victory in the Mobil 1 Ford.

After 15 events the NASCAR Winston Cup points leaders were: Bobby Labonte, 2240; Dale Earnhardt, 2183; Dale Jarrett, 2125; Ward Burton, 2096 and Jeff Burton, 2019.

NASCAR Winston Cup Race 16
Save Mart/Kragen 350
Sears Point Raceway
June 25, 2000

JEFF GORDON COMES THROUGH AT SEARS POINT, HIS SIXTH RACE COURSE VICTORY IN A ROW

Jeff Gordon is so good on road courses that former World Champion Jackie Stewart would have been happy to have him as a driver on his Formula One team. So good that had he not won here today in the first road course event of 2000, his season might have been considered a failure. Gordon, piloting the DuPont Chevrolet, admitted that he and his team were under "a lot of pressure." The three-time Winston Cup winner did pull off the victory by a comfortable 4.101 seconds over Sterling Marlin in the Coors Chevrolet who was having his best ever road course run. Marlin is best noted for his ability to eke out superior fuel mileage on superspeedways on the way to wins in 500 mile events. Mark Martin, another of NASCAR's road racing stars, in the Valvoline Ford, finished third, followed by Bobby Labonte and Ricky Rudd. Gordon became the fourth two-time winner of 2000, but languished near the bottom of the year's top 10 in points. Rusty Wallace, also an accomplished road racer claimed the pole but finished way back in the pack.

Jeff Gordon races toward his sixth road course victory in a row

Nigel Kinrade

Nigel Kinrade

NASCAR Winston Cup Race 17
Pepsi 400
Daytona International Speedway
July 1, 2000

FORD DOMINATES DAYTONA AGAIN, JEFF BURTON BESTS DALE JARRETT

Night or day it seemed to make no difference as Fords filled the top five finishing slots at Daytona under lights on a July evening just as they did in February's sunshine. This time leader Jeff Burton was on top at the end, successfully blocking February victor Jarrett from his strong bid to take both Daytona outings of 2000. Jarrett was again on the pole and might have won again except for one slow pit stop with a lug nut problem that dropped him from the lead to 27th place. Rusty Wallace, Mark Martin and Jarrett teammate Ricky Rudd, the second fastest qualifier, completed the all-Ford top five. Sixth place Tony Stewart drove the first Pontiac finisher, while Dale Earnhardt, in eighth place, had the best Chevrolet. Bill Elliott was a major factor until being punted into the wall by Mike Skinner. Burton's margin of victory was a slim .149 seconds.

The Winston Cup points leaders after 17 events were: Bobby Labonte, 2574; Dale Earnhardt, 2475; Dale Jarrett, 2451; Ward Burton, 2347 and Jeff Burton, 2314.

NASCAR Winston Cup Race 18
thatlook.com 300
New Hampshire International Raceway
July 9, 2000

NO JOY IN TONY STEWART'S RAIN SHORTENED THIRD WIN OF THE YEAR AT NEW HAMPSHIRE

The skies were grey, matching the mood of the Winston Cup fraternity when race leader Tony Stewart, in the Home Depot Pontiac, took the checkered flag 27 laps short of the scheduled 300 due to the day's second downfall. The somber mood reflected the loss of Sabco Racing's driver Kenny Irwin in a practice crash two days earlier. Stewart's third win, the most of any driver in 2000, should have been cause for celebration but even the post-race festivities were skipped. Joe Nemechek, in the Oakwood Homes Chevrolet, had one of his better outings, taking runner-up honors. Mark Martin, in the Valvoline Ford, started third, finished in the same slot, ahead of Jerry Nadeau and Jeff Gordon. Rusty Wallace collected pole honors for the seventh time in 2000, topping the charts, but again failed to capitalize, finishing 15th. In a touch of irony, runner-up Nemechek won at New Hampshire in the Sabco Chevrolet after being dismissed in favor of Irwin. Points leader Bobby Labonte finished ninth but lost little ground to second place Dale Earnhardt who finished only two slots ahead of him today.

NASCAR Winston Cup Race 19
Pennsylvania 500
Pocono Raceway
July 23, 2000

RUSTY WALLACE PREVAILS AT POCONO WHEN TEAMMATE JEREMY MAYFIELD FALTERS

Jeremy Mayfield was two corners away from victory in the Pennsylvania 500 when the right front tire on his Mobil 1 Ford blew. The mishap let teammate Rusty Wallace, in Miller livery, cruise by for the win. Mayfield won the year's previous Pocono race when he was the beneficiary of a last lap incident. Winner Wallace did not start on the pole but occupied the outside front row position. He spent the closing stages of the race fending off Jeff Burton to maintain second place, an accomplishment that paid off handsomely. Jeff Gordon nailed down third place. Fourth place Dale Jarrett, who led the most laps, 73, lost his chance at the victory. He alone of the leaders, elected to take on four tires on the last pit stop, the others gambling on two.

Polesitter Tony Stewart lost a lap to tire problems and ended up 26th. He won both Pocono outings in his rookie 1999 year. Matt Kenseth, leading a hot Rookie of the Year contest, occupied the last slot in the day's top five.

NASCAR Winston Cup Race 20
Brickyard 400
Indianapolis Motor Speedway
August 5, 2000

BIG DAY FOR BOBBY LABONTE AS HE WINS THE BRICKYARD 400

He'd been close before, second, third, and second, in three previous tries, but never before had he won the Brickyard 400. It's the only NASCAR race at the huge Indianapolis Motor Speedway, which routinely turns out 350,000 fans for the event. Labonte's new found patience paid off. For almost 100 laps he followed Rusty Wallace's leading Ford around, probing for an opening that never appeared. Wallace led 110 of the 160 laps but once Labonte got by on lap 146 and into clean air the Pontiac driver built up a substantial 4.229 second margin at the checker. Labonte and Wallace were the class of the field. Nobody else came close, not even about to retire Darrell Waltrip, who surprised everybody by qualifying second fastest after struggling all year to make the field. Waltrip finished 11th, his best result in a long time. He might even have made the top 10 with a little better performance from his pit crew.

"I would have been heartbroken if I would have finished second today," said Labonte post-race. Instead, the heartbreak went to Wallace, now the only driver other than Labonte to have finished second twice. Wallace told the story of the race succinctly. "I just couldn't shake him." A pit row collision cost him the win in '95, which went to Dale Earnhardt. Bill Elliott, Jerry Nadeau and Tony Stewart completed the top five but they were never truly in the hunt for the victory.

Nigel Kinrade

Nigel Kinrade

rewarding since it proved his ability to return to the top level after a serious crash early in his rookie year of 1998. Jeff Burton, Robby Gordon and pole winner Bobby Labonte rounded out the top five. The Gordon with the sterling road racing credentials, Jeff, had an off day on the 2.45 mile road course, where he had won the three previous races, starting eighth and finishing 23rd.

NASCAR Winston Cup Race 22
Pepsi 400 presented by Meijer
Michigan International Speedway
August 20, 2000

RUSTY WALLACE MASTERS MICHIGAN IN A REVERSAL OF LUCK

No, he wasn't on the pole this time out as he had been seven times previously this year, but he was in the winner's circle, a vastly more rewarding piece of real estate. Rusty Wallace had been unable to convert any of his year 2000 poles into wins, but a 10th place starting slot worked just fine at Michigan's Pepsi 400. Dale Earnhardt Jr. took pole honors but finished 31st, a lap down. Even that was better than half brother Kenny's accident shortened effort. Wallace first got the lead on lap 27, trading it with Ricky Rudd and Bobby Labonte on the basis of tire strategy as much as outright speed. Wallace's crew made the right call on the last stop, four tires, enabling him to get past Rudd, still looking for his first victory of the year, who took on only two. Rudd was 2.971 seconds behind at the finish, followed by Labonte, 1999 Cup winner Dale Jarrett and Johnny Benson. Wallace became the only three-time winner this year. Coupled with a pair of Mayfield victories, the Penske South Racing group has the most of any team, beating Joe Gibbs' pair by one. Part of that success is credited to Penske's engine building operation which is rumored to turn out more horsepower than any other.

NASCAR Winston Cup Race 21
Global Crossing @ The Glen
Watkins Glen International
August 14, 2000

STEVE PARK NOTCHES HIS FIRST WINSTON CUP VICTORY AT WATKINS GLEN

It wasn't a banner day for Dale Earnhardt the driver. He backed his Goodwrench Chevrolet into the barrier on the second lap and finished a lowly 25th. But for Dale Earnhardt Inc. celebration was very much in order. Steve Park, the second driver on his team, scored his first Winston Cup victory in the Pennzoil Chevrolet on his "home" track making Earnhardt's new team an unqualified success with the season only half over. Dale Earnhardt Jr., the team's other driver, has already posted two wins - and how many new teams can boast three in their first season? Park clearly earned top honors. He led 54 of the final 61 laps. Park's closest pursuer was Mark Martin, and he wasn't that close, 4.229 seconds behind at the finish. Team owner Earnhardt has proved adept at recruiting technical as well as driving talent, picking up respected veteran Steve Hmiel after he left Roush Racing and Paul Andrews from Penske Kranefuss Racing. Park's victory was particularly

NASCAR Winston Cup Race 23
goracing.com 500
Bristol Motor Speedway
August 27, 2000

RUSTY WALLACE MAKES IT TWO IN A ROW AT BRISTOL

Rusty Wallace nailed down his eighth pole and his fourth victory of the year at Bristol, the first outing in which he was able to make the no. 1 starting position stick. Post-race Wallace noted, "I just love Bristol." He should, he has now won three of the last four races and five of the past eight poles at the tricky high-banked half mile. Wallace got his toughest opposition from Tony Stewart with whom he alternated in the lead. Wallace's crew got him out ahead of Stewart on the final pit stop and all the polesitter had to do was catch Ward Burton who had gambled on a two tire stop. Burton's gamble failed. He was an easy Wallace victim

and Stewart, hampered by lapped traffic, grazed the wall trying to catch up. This left Wallace a free ride to victory lane with a .501 second margin at the end. Mark Martin, Dale Earnhardt and Steve Park rounded out the top five.

After 23 races the Winston Cup points leaders were: Bobby Labonte, 3458; Dale Jarrett, 3367; Dale Earnhardt, 3263; Jeff Burton, 3230 and Rusty Wallace, 3168.

NASCAR Winston Cup Race 24
Pepsi Southern 500
Darlington Raceway
September 3, 2000

WINNER BOBBY LABONTE GETS A LUCKY BREAK IN THE RAIN SHORTENED SOUTHERN 500

Everything seemed to be going against Bobby Labonte at Darlington. He destroyed his primary car in practice due to a stuck throttle and had to go to a back up car, and a provisional 37th place starting position. To top it off he was stuck with an undesireable pit position at the head of pit row. The latter turned out to be a blessing. Over a long afternoon Labonte got into contention. Then, after a late caution due to Jerry Nadeau's blown engine, Labonte's sharp crew got him out in the lead and the rains came. From nowhere Labonte was the winner of a six hour and 15 minute endurance contest punctuated by a two hour rain delay. His "we were blessed" post-race observation was an understatement. Jeff Burton, Dale Earnhardt, Jeff Gordon and Dale Jarrett were bunched up behind him when the event was called after 328 laps. It wasn't the longest Southern 500 on record. The 1951 event went six hours and 30 minutes - with no rain delays. Herb Thomas' winning payout was $8,000 compared to Labonte's take of $198,180.

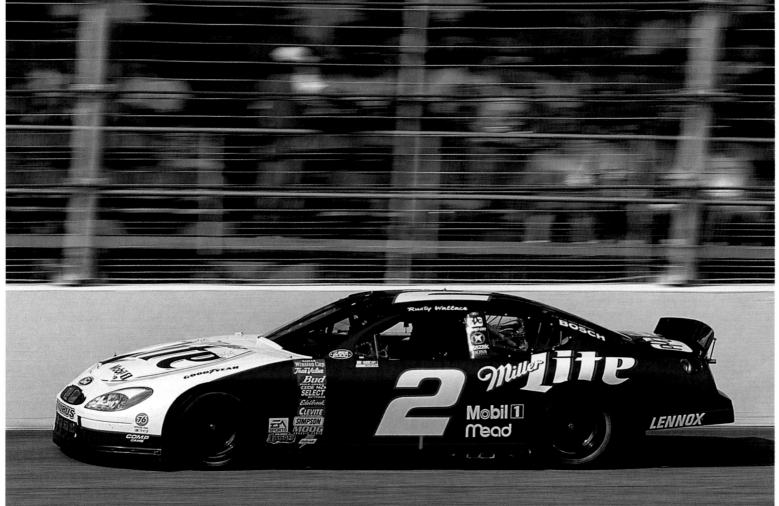

Nigel Kinrade

Nigel Kinrade

NASCAR Winston Cup Race 25
Chevrolet Monte Carlo 400
Richmond International Raceway
September 9, 2000

JEFF GORDON GETS THE VICTORY AT RICHMOND

"One of my best ever," said Jeff Gordon of his 52nd career victory on the three-quarter mile Richmond oval. Rusty Wallace was the dominant driver in the first half of the event but dropped out with a blown engine. Gordon's pit crew then handed him a great stop good for second place. On the restart after a final caution he passed pole winner and leader Jeff Burton and held on for the final five laps. Though challenged, Gordon resisted a charge by Dale Earnhardt on fresh tires that netted second place. Mark Martin and Steve Park also got past Burton in the final stages demoting the Exide Batteries Ford driver to fifth place at the end. Gordon's third win of 2000 with his new crew was not unblemished. NASCAR inspectors impounded his manifold for possible violations. Gordon's fans, however, were happy to seem him win on an oval. They take road course victories more or less for granted.

NASCAR Winston Cup Race 26
Dura Lube 300
New Hampshire International Speedway
September 17, 2000

JEFF BURTON LEADS EVERY LAP IN THE DURA LUBE 300

He wasn't on the pole but Jeff Burton, in the Exide Batteries Ford, led the first lap of the Dura Lube 300 and all those remaining. This feat was last accomplished by Cale Yarborough in June 1978 in Nashville. Pole winner Bobby Labonte followed him around for second place. The race ended under caution and was stopped by a red flag for clean up of a John Andretti triggered multicar accident. The race was the first restrictor plate event other than those on the two and a half mile superspeedways. The restrictor plate ruling was NASCAR's response to the two deaths at New Hampshire this year. It did slow the field somewhat but may have contributed to a definite lack of excitement. Ricky Rudd, Dale Jarrett and Rusty Wallace completed the top five. Burton's win moved him into the Winston Cup points runner-up slot, but still 168 points behind leader Labonte.

NASCAR Winston Cup Race 27
MBNA.com 400
Dover Downs International Speedway
September 24, 2000

TONY STEWART RUNS AWAY FROM THE DOVER DOWNS FIELD FOR VICTORY NO. 4

Tony Stewart, in the Home Depot Pontiac, started far back in 27th place but he was a huge 6.752 seconds ahead of runner-up Johnny Benson at the finish of Dover Downs' MBNA.com 400. He led four times for 163 of the 400 laps before a sellout crowd estimated at 130,000. Teammate Bobby Labonte made progress, too. His fifth place left him with a 158 point lead in the Winston Cup race over Dale Earnhardt, 17th today. Points pursuers Jeff Burton, who crashed, and Dale Jarrett, who didn't, had unhappy outings, ending up 36th and 32nd. Johnny Benson, still looking for a win, brought the Aaron Rents Pontiac home second. Ricky Rudd, still looking for a year 2000 win, placed third, followed by Steve Park.

NASCAR Winston Cup Race 28
NAPA AutoCare 500
Martinsville Speedway
October 1, 2000

TONY STEWART MAKES IT TWO IN A ROW AT MARTINSVILLE

Tony Stewart maintained his recent torrid pace with his second victory in two weeks. At Martinsville, he started on the pole but Jeff Burton had the second half of the race under control spinning off 108 consecutive laps in the lead. That advantage was cancelled when he had to back off for Jeff Gordon exiting the pits after a yellow on lap 467. That incident handed the lead to Tony Stewart who maintained it til the end. Dale Earnhardt in a late race charge also got past Burton for runner-up honors. Ricky Rudd was fourth and Jeff Gordon, the beneficiary of a two tire final stop, claimed the final spot in the top five. Stewart's fifth win of the year makes him the league leader in the victory column and elevates him into the top five in the Winston Cup points standings.

Nigel Kinrade

Nigel Kinrade

NASCAR Winston Cup Race 29
UAW-GM Quality 500
Lowe's Motor Speedway
October 8, 2000

BOBBY LABONTE SOLIDIFIES HIS TITLE CLAIM WITH VICTORY AT LOWE'S

With only five events remaining on the 2000 schedule Bobby Labonte left Lowe's Motor Speedway with the UAW-GM Quality 500 winner's trophy and a 252 point lead over Jeff Burton in the title chase. He started on the front row, was never out of contention and romped home with a 1.163 second margin of victory over Jeremy Mayfield in the Mobil 1 Ford.

Pole winner Jeff Gordon was not so lucky. He was taken out of the contest after only 53 laps by an accident. What could have been a victory turned into a lowly 39th place. Jeremy Mayfield collected runner-up honors ahead of Ricky Rudd with his fourth top five finish in a row. Labonte teammate Tony Stewart didn't post a third consecutive win but his fourth place

added useful points in his bid to stay in the year's top five. Mark Martin finished fifth, while championship contender Dale Earnhardt took down 11th place.

The NASCAR Winston Cup points leaders following the 29th event were: Bobby Labonte, 4405; Dale Earnhardt, 4153; Dale Jarrett, 4147; Jeff Burton, 4017 and Tony Stewart, 3977.

NASCAR Winston Cup Race 30
Winston 500
Talladega Superspeedway
October 15, 2000

"INCREDIBLE" DALE EARNHARDT TAKES TALLADEGA BY STORM

Dale Earnhardt hates restrictor plates but he loves Talladega, where the unpopular devices are mandatory. With his victory in the Winston 500 he has now won three of the last four races on NASCAR's

biggest superspeedway - this one worth an extra $1 million in Winston bonus money. The manner in which he put his stamp on the track that has been the scene of numerous multicar wrecks can only be described as incredible. He started 20th and, with five laps to go, was seemingly out of contention in 18th place. Somehow the master of the draft sliced through the pack rapidly enough to spend the last lap fighting off Kenny Wallace in the Square D Chevrolet from his vulnerable position in the lead. He had only a .119 second lead at the finish, but it was enough to garner him a standing ovation from the crowd. His log book now shows 10 Talladega victories, a figure unmatched by any other driver. Pole winner Joe Nemechek garnered third place followed by the Hendrick Motorsports pair of Jeff Gordon and Terry Labonte. Earnhardt teammate Mike Skinner was the seventh place runner, as Chevrolets blanketed the leader board. Rusty Wallace, in eighth place, had the top Ford. Earnhardt is noted for amazing feats of derring do but he'll have to go a long way to top today's virtuoso performance.

Jeremy Mayfield. Bobby Labonte, who could have played it safe, instead "came to race," and notched a worthwhile fourth place. His 165 points were more than enough to secure the Winston Cup with one more race still on the schedule. Gibbs was ecstatic,

Atlanta Motor Speedway
November 20, 2000

JERRY NADEAU GETS HIS BREAKTHROUGH FIRST VICTORY AT ATLANTA

marked by running out of money himself or driving for cash strapped teams, Nadeau, in his Chevrolet, was in a different league this year. His $180,550 race purse pushed his season winnings over $2 million.

ner-up, 2.197 seconds behind Jarrett. A consistent Ricky Rudd took down third place, followed by Jeff Burton and Rusty Wallace. Skilled qualifier Jeremy Mayfield put another pole into

with 20 laps to go when disaster struck. The Pontiacs of Rick Mast and Mike Bliss collided heavily in front of him. With nowhere to go Rudd's Ford tagged Bliss' Pontiac and a near cer-

2000 NASCAR Craftsman Truck Series Champion Greg Biffle

NASCAR Craftsman Truck Series

Ford Drivers Greg Biffle and Kurt Busch Run Away with the Top Honors

Roush Racing drivers Greg Biffle and Kurt Busch romped through the NASCAR Craftsman Truck campaign to take nine wins and top honors. Biffle, with five, got the championship, denied him in 1999 by a penalty for a mechanical violation. Busch, the season's sensation, scored four wins, placed second in the series and easily won the Rookie of the Year title. He displayed such talent that owner Jack Roush promoted him directly to the Winston Cup Series for 2001. Biffle was rewarded with a Busch Series ride. Biffle and Busch were highly competent qualifiers, each scoring four poles. Ford secured it's first Driver's Championship in the Truck Series and its second Manufacturer's Championship in a row. Biffle's title wasn't all a stroll in the park. He didn't get his first win of the year until May at Fountain, Colorado, and added three of the next four to his victory total. Busch could have been the winner at Sparta, Kentucky but ruined his chances in a burst of rookie enthusiasm. He first won at Milwaukee and then at Loudon, New Hampshire, the following week. Biffle nemesis Jack Sprague, the defending champion, had his chances at a repeat title with three victories, but crashed out in five

races and had mechanical problems in one. The Chevrolet driver finished a well beaten but respectable fifth in the points. One of Sprague's accidents was in the season opener at Daytona, the series' first venture onto a super-speedway. Veteran Geoffrey Bodine was the principal victim of a heart-

NASCAR CRAFTSMAN TRUCK SERIES			
DRIVER	PTS.	WINS	POLES
GREG BIFFLE	3826	5	4
KURT BUSCH	3596	4	4
ANDY HOUSTON	3566	2	1
MIKE WALLACE	3450	2	2
JACK SPRAGUE	3316	3	
JOE RUTTMAN	3278	3	8
DENNIS SETZER	3214	1	
RANDY TOLSMA	3157	1	
BRYAN REFFNER	3153	1	2
STEVE GRISSOM	3113		

stopping multiple truck accident on Daytona's fast back stretch. He attributed his survival and relatively minor injuries to his special attention to safety items like helmet, seat belts and roll cages. Andy Houston notched two victories and third place in the Series. Fourth place Mike Wallace matched him in wins and top fives (13) but was two down in top 10s with

16. Wallace with two poles, out-qualified Houston with one. No youngster, but as competitive as ever, Joe Ruttman won three times and just missed the year's top five. He was the year's top qualifier, notching eight poles, twice as many as the next best driver. A three-time winner and the third highest points producer in 1999, Dennis Setzer, had a disappointing year, dropping to seventh place in 2000 on the basis of only a single victory. Eighth place Randy Tolsma notched his first win since 1997 and moved into the top 10 for the first time. Benefitting from first class equipment Bryan Reffner not only won his first truck race, but captured a pair of poles as well, on his way to ninth place in the points parade. Steve Grissom made the year's top 10 without winning a race or a pole but placing in the top five a half dozen times. Outside the year's top 10, the only race winners were Rick Carelli on the comeback trail and Winston Cupper Bobby Hamilton, an occasional starter. Sophomore Jamie McMurray was not a race winner, but impressed tracksiders by winning a pair of poles. With more consistency he could be a contender. On a note of good cheer for the Series, Craftsman announced a five year extension of its role as title sponsor.

Ronda Greer

1 Denied in 1999 by a penalty, **GREG BIFFLE** nailed down the NASCAR Craftsman Truck title with five victories and a clear margin over teammate Kurt Busch. He goes to the Busch Series in 2001. (3826 NASCAR Craftsman Truck points)

Ronda Greer

2 Sensational newcomer **KURT BUSCH** earned runner-up honors and the Rookie of the Year title. Jack Roush promoted him directly to his Winston Cup team. (3596 NASCAR Craftsman Truck points)

3 Best year yet for **ANDY HOUSTON** who clinched third place in the series with two wins. He was out of the top 10 only six times. (3566 NASCAR Craftsman Truck points)

4 Daytona winner **MIKE WALLACE** added one other victory, was a consistent front runner. (3450 NASCAR Craftsman Truck points)

5 What could have been a third title for **JACK SPRAGUE** with three victories was lost in a costly run of crashes. (3316 NASCAR Craftsman Truck points)

6 Daytona pole winner **JOE RUTTMAN** was as competitive as ever with three victories. More consistency was needed to go higher. (3278 NASCAR Craftsman Truck points)

7 **DENNIS SETZER** scored a single victory, down from three in 1999, dropped four places in the rankings. (3214 NASCAR Craftsman Truck points)

8 **RANDY TOLSMA** made the top 10 on the basis of one win, six top fives and 15 top 10s. (3157 NASCAR Craftsman Truck points)

9 Pole winner at the Texas finale, **BRYAN REFFNER** won the race as well for a breakthrough victory and a ninth place for the season. (3153 NASCAR Craftsman Truck points)

10 The only one of the year's top 10 without a victory, **STEVE GRISSOM** was still a regular front runner. (3113 NASCAR Craftsman Truck points)

NASCAR Craftsman Truck Race 1
Daytona 250
Daytona International Speedway
February 18, 2000

MIKE WALLACE AVOIDS A 13 TRUCK WRECK, WINS AT DAYTONA

When Joe Ruttman qualified his Dodge truck on the pole at 187.563 mph, not that much slower than Dale Jarrett's Daytona 500 pole winning speed of 191.091 in his Ford Taurus Winston Cup car, spectators at Daytona's first Truck Series race knew they were in for some excitement. More excitement than they bargained for, as a harrowing 13 truck wreck on the backstretch mid-race sent Geoffrey Bodine's Ford tumbling and airborne. Unbelievably he wasn't critically injured but admitted that "I've never had a wreck like that in my life." When racing resumed after a two hour delay, Mike Wallace held off hard charging rookie Kurt Busch and Andy Houston for the win. Terry Cook and Kenny Martin rounded out the top five. The Truck Series' first outing on a two and a half mile superspeedway proved to be fast and competitive, for vehicles that lack the aerodynamic sophistication of the Winston Cup sedans.

NASCAR Craftsman Truck Race 2
Florida Dodge Dealers 400K
Homestead-Miami Speedway
February 26, 2000

ANDY HOUSTON DOMINATES THE DODGE DEALERS 400K

Andy Houston had a near miss in the season opener at Daytona, but made no mistakes this time, as he cruised home 4.506 seconds ahead of Mike Wallace, who beat him at Daytona on the last lap. Wallace won a bruising battle for runner-up honors with 1999 champion Jack Sprague, Joe Ruttman, again the pole winner, and Greg Biffle, who finished in that order. Houston was the big beneficiary of this battle behind him since none of the quartet could concentrate on running him down.

NASCAR Craftsman Truck Race 3
Chevy Trucks NASCAR 150
Phoenix International Raceway
March 18, 2000

POLE WINNER JOE RUTTMAN CAPTURES THE CHEVY TRUCKS 150

Fifty-five year old Joe Ruttman and his DANA Dodge are fast. They have been on the pole for all three NASCAR Craftsman Truck races this year. At Phoenix, Ruttman made it stick, in a hotly contested battle with Jack Sprague for top honors that gave him a .237 margin over the Chevrolet driver at the finish. Andy Houston, the Homestead-Miami winner, was the third finisher followed by Kurt Busch, well in the lead for the Rookie of the Year title and his Roush Racing teammate Greg Biffle. A modest Ruttman was thrilled that "the young guys let me win."

NASCAR Craftsman Truck Race 4
Dodge California Truck Stop 250
Mesa Marin Raceway
March 26, 2000

MIKE WALLACE GETS HIS SECOND WIN OF 2000 FROM THE POLE

Mike Wallace turned his first pole of 2000 into his second win of the year and the Truck Series points leadership. Joe Ruttman and Randy Renfrow were battling for the lead with nine laps to go when lapped traffic caused Ruttman to spin and Renfrow to lose momentum. In third place at the time, Wallace made the pass and cruised home with a .345 second margin of victory. He left the track with a 16 point edge over Andy Houston in the Craftsman Truck point standings. Kurt Busch, Jack Sprague and Steve Grissom also took advantage of Houston's misfortune which left him in fifth place at the end.

After four rounds the points leaders were: Mike Wallace, 675; Andy Houston, 659; Kurt Busch, 643; Greg Biffle, 587 and Joe Ruttman, 581.

NASCAR Craftsman Truck Race 5
NAPA 250
Martinsville Speedway
April 10, 2000

BOBBY HAMILTON NAILS THE VICTORY IN THE NAPA 250

Rain delayed the NAPA 250 at Martinsville on Sunday but nothing delayed Winston Cupper Bobby Hamilton on Monday when competition restarted. Mike Wallace, the Mesa Marin winner, again took the pole in his Ford but couldn't hold off Dodge mounted Hamilton who was making one of his rare Truck starts. Hamilton's margin of victory was a very convincing 4.354 seconds. Runner-up Wallace could take some consolation in the Craftsman Truck points lead, now up to 59 over Andy Houston who finished outside the top 10 today. 1999 champion Jack Sprague, was in the first Chevrolet to finish, notched third place over Dennis Setzer and Steve Grissom, the other members of the top five.

NASCAR Craftsman Truck Race 6
Line-X 225
Portland International Speedway
April 22, 2000

ANDY HOUSTON BOUNCES BACK FOR THE LINE-X 225 WIN

Andy Houston bounced back from an early race tangle with Mike Wallace to capture the Line-X 225. The mishap shuffled both back to mid-pack but sharp pit work

and diligent driving positioned Houston on leader Dennis Setzer's tailgate on the last lap. Houston squeezed his Chevrolet past Setzer's Dodge in a tight turn and motored off to a 1.616 second margin of victory. Jack Sprague, Mike Wallace and Rick Crawford completed the top five. Pole winner Greg Biffle failed to make good on his qualifying speed and finished outside the top 10.

NASCAR Craftsman Truck Race 7
RAM Tough 200 by Pepsi
Gateway International Raceway
May 7, 2000

1999 CHAMPION JACK SPRAGUE SCORES AT GATEWAY

Two-time Truck champion Jack Sprague scored his first victory of 2000 in the RAM Tough 200 in convincing fashion. His Chevrolet was a huge 7.032 seconds in front of runner-up Jimmy Hensley, also Chevrolet mounted, at the finish. As he had in the previous Portland round, Ford protagonist Greg Biffle won the pole. He ended up fourth this time out, behind the Dodge driven by Randy Tolsma and ahead of Joe Ruttman's Dodge.

NASCAR Craftsman Truck Race 8
Quaker State 200
Memphis Motorsports Park
May 13, 2000

JACK SPRAGUE MAKES IT TWO IN A ROW AT MEMPHIS

Jack Sprague was the beneficiary of leader Greg Biffle's bobble on the last lap and inherited the win, his second in a row. Biffle blamed his misstep on a slick spot on the track, not to any pressure from Sprague. He recovered to finish a disappointed runner-up. Sprague's good luck moved him into second place in the championship chase. Dennis Setzer managed third place, followed by Mike Wallace and Steve Grissom. Pole winner Bobby Hamilton failed to finish in the top 10.

NASCAR Craftsman Truck Race 9
Grainger.com 200
Pikes Peak International Raceway
May 21, 2000

GREG BIFFLE GETS HIS FIRST WIN OF 2000 IN THE GRAINGER.COM 200

Winless in 2000, the winningest driver of 1999 scored his first victory of the year in the Grainger.com 200. Fittingly enough his Ford is also sponsored by Grainger. Roush Racing teammate Kurt Busch followed him across the line. Pole winner Andy Houston notched third place while fourth finisher Jack Sprague took over the series points lead. Previous top man Mike Wallace had an unhappy outing ending up in the wall. Fifth place went to Dennis Setzer.

After nine rounds the NASCAR Craftsman Truck points leaders were: Jack Sprague, 1434; Mike Wallace, 1378; Greg Biffle, 1362; Andy Houston, 1353 and Steve Grissom, 1282.

NASCAR Craftsman Truck Race 10
Sears 200
Evergreen Speedway
June 3, 2000

JACK SPRAGUE SAILS TO VICTORY IN THE SEARS 200

A lap down due to replacing a cut tire Jack Sprague got all the way back up to third place by dint of brilliant driving. Winning took a little luck. He then banged into a lapped truck bringing out the yellow. During the caution he stayed out while leader Randy Tolsma and second place Joe Ruttman pitted. Chevrolet driver Sprague then held off the Dodge pair of former front runners to score the victory by a margin of .221 seconds. The Roush pair of Greg Biffle and Kurt Busch filled out the top five in the Sears 200.

NASCAR Craftsman Truck Race 11
Pronto Auto Parts 400
Texas Motor Speedway
June 9, 2000

GREG BIFFLE WINS FROM THE POLE AT TEXAS

A back in form Greg Biffle dominated a rain delayed Pronto Auto Parts 400. He led 119 of 167 laps from the pole. He held off Mike Wallace and Randy Tolsma after a late race restart to arrive first at the finish with a 2.741 margin of victory. Andy Houston and Bryan Reffner rounded out the top five. Arch rival Jack Sprague went into the wall late in the race and out of the points lead which fell to Biffle.

NASCAR Craftsman Truck Race 12
Kroger 225
Kentucky Speedway
June 17, 2000

GREG BIFFLE CAPTURES THE KROGER 225

Displaying the form that made him the biggest winner of 1999, Greg Biffle notched his third victory of the year in the Kroger 225 on the new 1.5 mile Kentucky oval. Bryan Reffner won the pole but could manage only fifth position at the finish. Jack Sprague recovered from his Texas misfortune to claim runner-up honors, 2.182 seconds in arrears. Mike Wallace and Marty Houston filled the third and fourth finishing slots. The race was delayed by rain for over an hour. When it restarted under yellow Biffle pitted and with the good luck inherent in subsequent caution laps was able to sneak home without making another pit stop.

NASCAR Craftsman Truck Race 13
Bully Hill Vineyards 150
Watkins Glen International
June 24, 2000

THREE IN A ROW FOR GREG BIFFLE. HE WINS WATKINS GLEN FROM THE POLE

Road racer Ron Fellows provided all the excitement on the winding 2.45 mile upstate New York circuit, coming from last to third on the final lap in his Chevrolet. He put some pressure on leader Greg Biffle's Ford but not enough to upset him and teammate Kurt Busch. The Roush pair finished one-two comfortably ahead of the road racing star. The Bully Hill Vineyards 150 registered as Biffle's third win in a row and firmly established him on his perch atop the NASCAR Craftsman Truck Series points. Pleased with his fine run, Fellows was philosophic, "Who knows? In a couple more laps, I might have made it. But it was only 62." Mike Wallace and Jack Sprague completed the top five.

NASCAR Craftsman Truck Race 14
Sears DieHard 200
The Milwaukee Mile
July 1, 2000

ROOKIE KURT BUSCH MASTERS MILWAUKEE

Promising rookie Kurt Busch made good on his promise by cracking the win column in the Sears DieHard 200 at Milwaukee's venerable mile. Moreover, he did it from the pole and broke teammate Greg Biffle's three race winning streak in the bargain. Biffle collected third place today behind runner-up Randy Tolsma. Retaining his comfortable points lead. Biffle had few regrets. Steve Grissom collected fourth place, ahead of Andy Houston. If Busch can temper his talent with a little patience he could be a title contender in his first year on the circuit.

NASCAR Craftsman Truck Race 15
thatlook.com 200
New Hampshire International Speedway
July 8, 2000

KURT BUSCH NAILS DOWN TWO IN A ROW AT NEW HAMPSHIRE

Starting his own mini-streak, Kurt Busch beat off a stern challenge from Mike Wallace, Randy Tolsma and Greg Biffle in the final countdown at New Hampshire to score his second win in a row. Wallace played bumper tag with Busch but had to be content with runner-up honors ahead of Tolsma and teammate Biffle. Andy Houston was the fifth driver in the day's top five. Team owner Jack Roush applauded Busch's new found maturity, "I was only hoping he'd be in contention to win late in the year." Pole winner Joe Ruttman finished out of the top 10.

NASCAR Craftsman Truck Race 16
Chevy Silverado 200
Nazareth Speedway
July 15, 2000

DENNIS SETZER NOTCHES HIS FIRST WIN OF THE YEAR AT NAZARETH

In the previous race at Nazareth, Dennis Setzer went home with a broken shoulder blade, incurred in a nasty crash. This time he went home with top honors and a genuine sense of relief at scoring his first victory of 2000 by a handsome margin of 2.057 seconds. Joe Ruttman captured the pole and runner-up honors but was no match for Setzer in the final countdown. Greg Biffle nailed down third place and kept his post at the top of the year's points leader board. Steve Grissom and 1999 champion Jack Sprague completed the top five. Third in the 1999 points chase, Setzer had been expected to be a factor in 2000 but was beleaguered by bad luck.

After 16 rounds the points were: Greg Biffle, 2582; Mike Wallace, 2404; Andy Houston, 2393; Jack Sprague, 2381 and Kurt Busch, 2320.

NASCAR Craftsman Truck Race 17
Michigan 200
Michigan Speedway
July 22, 2000

BACK ON TOP, GREG BIFFLE SCORES IN THE MICHIGAN 200

Denied the top spot by teammate Kurt Busch and Dennis Setzer for the last three races, Greg Biffle blasted his way into victory circle in the Michigan 200, padding his lead in the NASCAR Craftsman Truck points. Surprise pole winner Jamie McMurray managed sixth place at the finish. Biffle's teammate Kurt Busch was a well beaten runner-up, 1.324 seconds behind at the finish. Mike Wallace, pursuing Biffle in the points race, was the third place runner. Andy Houston and Dennis Setzer rounded out the top five.

NASCAR Craftsman Truck Race 18
Power Stroke 200
Indianapolis Raceway Park
August 3, 2000

JOE RUTTMAN PREVAILS FROM THE POLE IN THE POWER STROKE 200

Always a talented qualifier, Joe Ruttman isn't always able to capitalize on his pre-race speed. In the Power Stroke 200, however, he converted his pole position to the winner's podium, holding off runner-up Lyndon Amick by .859 second at the checkered flag. He led 152 of the 200 laps despite a confusing caution period that moved him out of the lead into mid-pack. When congratulated on his comeback he noted, "It's not my favorite thing to do." Third place Jamie McMurray had one of his better outings beating the two leading points producers No. 2 Mike Wallace and No. 1 Greg Biffle to the finish line.

NASCAR Craftsman Truck Race 19
Federated Auto Parts 250
Nashville Speedway USA
August 12, 2000

RANDY TOLSMA TAKES THE FEDERATED AUTO PARTS 250, HIS FIRST WIN IN THREE YEARS

Jack Sprague was in complete control of the Federated Auto Parts 250 for the first half of the race but suffered terminal engine trouble. Randy Tolsma was the beneficiary of Sprague's misfortune and led the final 112 laps to finish a scant .192 second in front of Dennis Setzer. Chad Chaffin claimed third place ahead of Joe Ruttman, the winner at IRP, and Steve Grissom. The winner was so appreciative that he threatened "to break down and cry my eyes out." Instead he cried all the way to the bank with his winner's check of $44,585. Jamie McMurray claimed another pole but was out before the halfway mark.

NASCAR Craftsman Truck Race 20
Sears Craftsman 175
Chicago Motor Speedway
August 27, 2000

JOE RUTTMAN RUNS OFF WITH VICTORY IN THE SEARS CRAFTSMAN 250

Roush Racing's Kurt Busch and Greg Biffle were the early front runners in the Sears Craftsman 175 but 55 year old Joe Ruttman supplied the finishing kick to end up in victory lane. Busch blew his chances with a bungled pit stop after a tangle with Jack Sprague that cost him two penalties. Biffle simply bobbled while in the lead letting Ruttman slip by for the win. Biffle admitted his error, "I just overran the corner," but recovered for second place. Mike Wallace placed third. Andy Houston and Rick Carelli completed the top five. Ruttman qualified on the pole and edged Biffle by .330 second at the end.

NASCAR Craftsman Truck Race 21
Kroger 200
Richmond International Raceway
September 7, 2000

RICK CARELLI COMES BACK TO VICTORY LANE IN THE KROGER 200

Rick Carelli was close to death after a wreck early in last year's campaign. Sixteen months later, in the Kroger 200, he proved that he could again be a winner. Pole winner Kurt Busch led the first half of the race before giving way to Joe Ruttman. Carelli then led twice, including the final 20 laps. Greg Biffle beat out teammate Busch for second place. Ruttman salvaged fourth place and Scott Riggs picked up the fifth finishing slot. An elated Carelli noted, "To come back and function at this level just shows that nothing's impossible."

NASCAR Craftsman Truck Race 22
MBNA e-commerce 200
Dover Downs International Speedway
September 22, 2000

KURT BUSCH BESTS MIKE WALLACE IN A HARD FOUGHT MBNA 200

Kurt Busch was on the pole, and on leader Mike Wallace's tailgate late in the MBNA e-commerce 200. Net result, Wallace went into the wall on the "Monster Mile" front straight and Busch went on to the winner's enclosure. Busch called the incident "just good hard racing." Wallace understandably begged to differ, citing Busch for lack of character. Greg Biffle also got by, picked up second place ahead of Rick Crawford. Andy Houston notched fourth place followed by Ken Schrader. Wallace was bounced all the way down to a 12th place finish. Busch, despite Wallace's objections, appears destined to take the runner-up honors in the NASCAR Craftsman Truck Series at year end.

NASCAR Craftsman Truck Race 23
O'Reilly 400
Texas Motor Speedway
October 13, 2000

BRYAN REFFNER'S BIG DAY: VICTORY IN THE O'REILLY 400, HIS FIRST POLE

It had been a long time since his debut in 1996, but Bryan Reffner finally got his breakthrough NASCAR Craftsman Truck Series victory. Moreover, he did it with a team he managed himself and garnered pole honors as well. Reffner had to beat off a determined Andy Houston in the final countdown, but prevailed by 1.277 seconds at the checker. He also cooled off red hot rookie Kurt Busch, winner of the Dover round, who slotted into third place. Always popular Jimmy Hensley managed fourth place ahead of Dennis Setzer. Reffner had survived some lean times in the series, so the victory was vindication for him and team owner John Menard, who backed him with first class equipment.

NASCAR Craftsman Truck Race 24
California 200
California Speedway
October 28, 2000

KURT BUSCH EXITS THE TRUCK SERIES IN STYLE WITH VICTORY IN CALIFORNIA

Kurt Busch capped his brief Truck Series career in style winning the season finale from the pole. His fourth win of the year propelled him into the Rookie of the Year title and second place in the season's standings behind Greg Biffle, the newly crowned champion, who placed fifth today. Andy Houston was the runner-up for the second race in a row, followed by Joe Ruttman and Jack Sprague. Busch was comfortably ahead until he bobbled on the last lap, but recovered to win by .775 second.

Ray Evernham and Richard Petty head the field of Dodge team owners.

Nigel Kinrade

Dodge Debut at Daytona 2001

What started as a skirmish by Ray Evernham's two car team has become a full scale invasion of Ford's and General Motors' NASCAR turf, as Dodge reenters the Winston Cup wars in force. Evernham has enlisted popular veteran Bill Elliott, a former champion, and promising rookie Casey Atwood as drivers. Petty Enterprises, with a history of Dodge successes, has entries for proven winners Kyle Petty and John Andretti as well as Buckshot Jones, who has some Winston Cup experience but not over a full season. Melling Racing goes with Stacy Compton. The owner of four championships in the CART series but a NASCAR newcomer, Chip Ganassi (with Felix Sabates) goes with Sterling Marlin, noted for his winning talents in 500 mile races, and rookie Jason Leffler, who had been scheduled for a Busch series ride with Jack Roush. With 10 Dodges entered and 40 Ford, Pontiac and Chevrolet combined entries Daytona will be particularly interesting. Since only 43 starting slots are available, some teams will be relegated to spectator roles.

Indy Racing Northern Light Series

A Deserving Champion, Buddy Lazier Takes the Indy Racing Northern Light Series Title

Out of the limelight since his heroic, pain-laced win in the Indy Racing League's first Indianapolis 500 in 1996, Buddy Lazier finally got the championship he deserved in 2000. Even beaten rival Eddie Cheever, who finished third in the title chase, gave him full marks. "He raced like a tiger all year and made my life miserable on the track. Off the track, he's a nice guy." The title was vindication, too, for Ron Hemelgarn, Lazier's only IRNLS car owner, whose faith that he was backing a champion never wavered. Lazier and Hemelgarn shrugged off an indifferent 1999 season when they went winless and luckless. It didn't take Lazier long to get into stride in 2000. An uncharacteristic mistake cost him the victory in the season opener at Orlando. Next time out, at Phoenix, he delivered a virtuoso performance coming from last on the starting grid in a back up car to take the win in commanding fashion. Las Vegas was a washout due to mechanical problems. Perhaps Lazier's finest outing came in a race he didn't win, the Indianapolis 500, but would have, except for the presence in the lineup of one Juan Pablo Montoya. Montoya waltzed away with top honors and a bag full of money in the employ of the CART champion Target/Ganassi Racing team. Lazier was the only serious opposition Montoya encountered all day. He finished second.

At the end of the season, 40 year old Scott Goodyear didn't drive like a man who had announced his imminent retirement. At the new Kentucky track he qualified on the pole, finished second to 2000 champion-to-be Lazier. In the season finale he reversed the numbers, taking the win from race runner-up Eddie Cheever. Cheever responded by offering points runner-up Goodyear a ride in his Infinity propelled team in 2001. Cheever will be remembered as the driver who delivered Infinity's first IRNLS victory in five years of trying in

the series dominated by Aurora. it took place at Pikes Peak and, added to Cheever's strong runner-up finish at Texas, led to the former Formula One pilot's third place in the season standings and positive outlook for 2001. Cheever's other podium finish of the year was third in the season opener at Orlando. Chilean Eliseo Salazar failed to win for car owner A.J. Foyt and garnered only one podium placement all year. That one, however, was at the Indianapolis 500, the race dear to Foyt, a four-time winner of the big event. Salazar did manage four top fives and a year end listing of fourth place in the points. The other member of the year's top five, Mark Dismore, failed to match his singleton win of 1999 and dropped two places in the standings despite a fine second place at Las Vegas. Sixth place Donnie Beechler actually matched fifth place Dismore's point production at 202 but lost the coveted top five placement on the basis of Dismore's highest finish (second) compared to his best outing (third). Beechler scored three top five race finishes.

The best race of the year, perhaps the IRNLS' best ever, Texas' Casino Magic 500, went to Scott Sharp over Robby McGehee by a slim .059 second margin. Sharp claimed another podium position at Pikes Peak, the next time out but those two would be the only ones of the year for the League's best financed team and one of its premier drivers. It all added up to seventh place in the year's standings for Sharp. Robbie Buhl's year got off to a great start with a come from behind victory in the Orlando season opener. No additional podium finishes turned up over the season, his first as a partial team owner, and his eighth place at year end failed to match a brilliant beginning.

Based on his record in Indy cars, unmatched by any other driver in the series, and his desire to get back to "his roots," the Indianapolis 500, Al Unser Jr.'s debut in the IRNLS was

disappointing. He did win at Las Vegas, but qualified only 18th at Indianapolis and was never a factor there. Two additional podium finishes enabled him to make the year's top 10, in ninth place.

Billy Boat salvaged a lackluster season with a podium finish in the year's final event, which enabled his placement in the year's top 10. After his own car failed to qualify for the Indianapolis 500, a courageous Boat finally made the field, literally at the last minute, in the third of a string of borrowed cars and finished a respectable 15th in the big race.

1999 champion Greg Ray suffered a reversal of fortune in 2000. The year's top qualifier garnered the pole in five of the year's nine events. In only one, Atlanta, could he convert his qualifying speed into victory. From topping the charts the previous year he ended up outside the top 10.

As usual, the Indianapolis 500 dwarfed every other event on the IRNLS schedule. What made it particularly intriguing this year was the invasion of uncharted turf by CART champion Target/Ganassi Racing and star drivers Juan Montoya and Jimmy Vasser. Montoya almost captured the pole, and smoothly ran away with the race by a clear seven seconds, leaving his only serious challenger, Buddy Lazier, a well beaten runner-up. Montoya's 167 laps in the lead were a measure of his virtuoso performance. In her sophomore year Sarah Fisher proved she could run with the big boys, making the podium for the first time at the new Kentucky track. It was no fluke, she qualified fourth fastest, and is also proving to be a genuine asset to the League.

A 13 race schedule in 2001 as opposed to nine in 2000 should be a major factor in the series development and real impetus could come if one or more major manufacturers decide to develop engines to the League's specifications.

1 A worthy champion, **BUDDY LAZIER** delivered vindication for long term car owner Ron Hemelgarn with his and the team's first title. Two wins, a pole and a pair of runner-up finishes, were the season's highlights. Fourth in the finale clinched top honors. (290 Indy Racing Northern Light Series points)

2 An announced retiree at the end of the year, 40 year old SCOTT GOODYEAR may have to change his mind on the basis of a sparkling victory in the year's last race. A pole winner in 2000, he has a firm offer for 2001. (272 Indy Racing Northern Light Series points)

3 Infinity protagonist **EDDIE CHEEVER** registered the first ever victory for the engine manufacturer at Pikes Peak. The 1998 Indianapolis 500 winner was competitive all year after a strong second place in the season opener. (257 Indy Racing Northern Light Series points)

4 **ELISEO SALAZAR** picked the right spot for his only podium finish of the year, the Indianapolis 500. He qualified third fastest as well, so the result was no fluke. (210 Indy Racing League Northern Light Series points)

5 Luck at Las Vegas **MARK DISMORE** captured the pole and runner-up honors at the nation's gambling capital. Luck elsewhere was missing. (202 Indy Racing Northern Light Series points)

6 **DONNIE BEECHLER**'s podium position at Phoenix was the highpoint of his season. It was one of three top fives for the year. (202 Indy Racing Northern Light Series points)

Indianapolis Motor Speedway/Roger Bedwell

Indianapolis Motor Speedway/Ron McQueeney

7 SCOTT SHARP, the winner of the year's best IRNLS race, scored at Texas in a classic duel with Robbie McGehee, followed his victory with third place at Pikes Peak. (196 Indy Racing Northern Light Series points)

8 A superb season start saw ROBBIE BUHL come from 22nd place at the start to the victory circle at Orlando. In the remaining eight races he registered only one additional top five. (190 Indy Racing Northern Light Series points)

Cheryl Day Anderson

Cheryl Day Anderson

9 Still a winner. AL UNSER, JR.'s victory at Las Vegas proved that the distinguished veteran could still find his way to the winner's enclosure. He made two other podiums but was uncompetitive in his favorite event, the Indianapolis 500. (188 Indy Racing Northern Light Series points)

10 BILLY BOAT scored his only podium finish of the year in the season's finale. He soldiered on through multiple setbacks during the season to make the top 10 list. (181 Indy Racing Northern Light Series points)

Eliseo Salazar, Juan Montoya, and pole winner Greg Ray occupy the front row for the start of the 2000 Indianapolis 500. Firestone's Al Speyer, white shirt, red hat and glasses between the Montoya and Ray cars, knows he has a winner. They're all on his tires.

The magnificent starting spectacle at the Indianapolis Motor Speedway soon gave way to serious racing. Montoya took over the lead from Ray on lap 27 and dominated the rest of the afternoon.

Indy Racing Northern Light Series Race 1
Delphi Indy 500
Walt Disney World Speedway
January 29, 2000

ROBBIE BUHL CARVES HIS WAY FROM 22nd TO FIRST IN ORLANDO SEASON OPENER

What better way to celebrate his debut as part owner of his own team than to win the year's first race. Robbie Buhl steered his way to victory circle from a way back 22nd place on the starting grid in the first race of the year. Buddy Lazier appeared to have the win in hand but made the one mistake that left him in second place at the end. 1999 champion Greg Ray took the pole but finished a lowly 17th. Eddie Cheever, Scott Goodyear and Eliseo Salazar scored the other top five finishes in that order.

Indy Racing Northern Light Series Race 2
MCI WorldCom Indy 200
Phoenix International Raceway
March 19, 2000

NO MISTAKES THIS TIME, BUDDY LAZIER SCORES AT PHOENIX

Phoenix has always been tough on Buddy Lazier. In 1996, he crashed in practice breaking his back. In 1999, he crashed again while running second. In 2000, his luck turned. From 26th and last on the starting grid he sliced his way through the field, owning a handsome 4.191 margin of victory over runner-up Scott Goodyear at the finish. Greg Ray was again the fastest qualifier, again failed to be a factor. Donnie Beechler notched the third podium spot, his first of the year. Eliseo Salazar and Scott Sharp completed the top five. Winner Lazier, on Firestone tires, along with the rest of the field in 2000, commented, "The tires were awesome." Lazier took the early season points lead.

Indy Racing Northern Light Series Race 3
Vegas Indy 300
Las Vegas Motor Speedway
April 22, 2000

AL UNSER JR. BACK IN VICTORY CIRCLE AT LAS VEGAS

Al Unser Jr. needed a little luck in the nation's casino capital to get back into victory circle for the first time since 1995. He got it in the form of smoke from the leading Dallara-Aurora of Scott Goodyear, who was black flagged handing the lead to Unser Jr. The other late race contender, Greg Ray, had already retired with gearbox troubles. Polesitter and eventual runner-up Mark Dismore was the victim of poor pit stop timing, was a huge 12.531 seconds behind Unser Jr. at the finish. Rookie Sam Hornish got a lot of pit row and spectator attention with his third place from 18th on the starting grid in a year old car. Jeret Schroeder and Robbie Buhl completed the top five. Even runner-up Dismore seemed to approve of the outcome. "I'm happy for little Al," he stated post-race.

Indy Racing Northern Light Series Race 4
Indianapolis 500
Indianapolis Motor Speedway
May 28, 2000

TARGET/GANASSI'S JUAN CARLOS MONTOYA MASTERS THE INDIANAPOLIS 500 HIS FIRST TIME OUT

In his first attempt to capture the pot of gold and the worldwide glory inherent in winning the Indianapolis 500, Juan Montoya succeeded in virtuoso style. Ignoring the warnings of Al Unser Jr. and others on the dangers lurking in the big, fast speedway, Montoya went calmly about doing what he does best, winning motor races. He started second easily bested pole winner Greg Ray early in the race and runner-up Buddy Lazier late in the long rain delayed afternoon. He led 167 of the 200 laps, the most of any driver in 30 years. A frustrated Ray crashed once, and, after a rebuild, crashed again. Montoya teammate Jimmy Vasser led briefly, ended up seventh, the victim of a failed pit stop strategy. Eliseo Salazar didn't win for car owner A.J. Foyt but his third place could not have left "Ol Tex" too unhappy. Jeff Ward and Eddie Cheever picked up the fourth and fifth finishing spots. The race boasted two lady starters, young Sarah Fisher and veteran Lyn St. James. Somehow they managed to tangle sending both into the wall. At the start of the day the crowd was hostile to Montoya, an invader from the rival CART circuit. By race end he had won their unequivocal admiration.

Indy Racing Northern Light Series Race 5
Casino Magic 500
Texas Motor Speedway
June 11, 2000

"IRNLS' BEST RACE EVER" GOES TO SCOTT SHARP

Young Robby McGehee made it close but Scott Sharp was in front by a car length, good for a .059 second margin, at the checker. For the last seven laps McGehee, seemingly faster, had done everything possible to dislodge leader Sharp but Sharp successfully blocked every move. With his rain delayed victory Sharp became the winningest IRNLS driver with a career five wins. Al Unser Jr. notched third place and admitted that he enjoyed watching the Sharp-McGehee tussle ahead, with no reasonable chance of catching either one of the flying pair. Earlier in the race Lazier and Unser had their own two man battle for the lead with Al Jr. prevailing. Buzz Calkins and Scott Goodyear completed the top five. McGehee has clearly shown his talent at the wheel. With better financing he would be a title contender.

Indy Racing Northern Light Series Race 6
Radisson Indy 200
Pikes Peak International Raceway
June 18, 2000

EDDIE CHEEVER DELIVERS INFINITY ITS FIRST VICTORY AT PIKES PEAK

Eddie Cheever had won before, but not Infinity, in five years of trying. Cheever's first win of 2000 was Infinity's first ever. Earlier, Infinity driver Robbie Buhl had led for 61 laps after qualifying second fastest but his Infinity expired. Two laps from the end Cheever was in command with Airton Dare in second place followed by Scott Sharp, Donnie Beechler and Mark Dismore. Al Unser Jr. then triggered a two car spin by tagging Beechler who hit the wall. The resulting yellow enabled Cheever to win under yellow, but he was so far ahead that he was not likely to be challenged. Sharp notched third place, followed by Dismore and the disabled Beechler. Cheever attributed the win to Infinity's favorable torque characteristics.

Indy Racing Northern Light Series Race 7
Midas Classic 500
Atlanta Motor Speedway
July 15, 2000

GREG RAY REBOUNDS TO SNARE THE ATLANTA WIN

Despite winning the pole in half of the year's previous races, 1999 champion Greg Ray had yet to make the top five, let alone win. His unhappy season turned brighter when he converted his fourth pole of 2000 into his first win of the year. No bad breaks this time. Ray was in charge all the way, even overcoming a pair of slow pit stops. Buddy Lazier and Al Unser Jr. battled for runner-up honors with the nod going to Unser. Robby McGehee and Donnie Beechler rounded out the top five.

Sarah Fisher's fine fifth place qualifying effort went for naught when she tagged the wall. Despite a late race caution that bunched the field, Ray enjoyed a 3.054 margin of victory along with a sigh of relief at the finish. Ray's qualifying speed of 216.101 mph was three miles per hour faster than that of next best Eliseo Salazar but IRNLS inspectors could find no infraction. Ray called it "attention to detail."

Indy Racing Northern Light Series Race 8
The Belterra Resort Indy 300
Kentucky Speedway
August 27, 2000

BUDDY LAZIER CLOSES IN ON IRNLS CHAMPIONSHIP WITH KENTUCKY SPEEDWAY

The handsome new Kentucky track proved to be just the right venue for 2000 IRNLS champion-to-be Buddy Lazier as he edged polesitter Scott Goodyear for his second victory of the year. A little luck as well as a great drive figured in the win, as Lazier's gearbox collapsed just as he reached the finish line, a mere 1.879 seconds ahead of Goodyear. Rookie Sam Hornish had a shot at winning, running 38 laps in the lead, before running out of fuel. Sophomore Sarah Fisher had the best day of her short career by qualifying fourth and finishing third, leading nine laps along the way, her first podium appearance. Eddie Cheever's solid fourth place kept him in the running for the championship. Stephan Gregoire hustled all the way up to fifth place from 21st on the starting grid.

The Kentucky event could have a long run on future IRNLS schedules if the inaugural is any indication. A reported crowd of 65,000 was enthusiastic and teams and drivers alike praised the layout. Having rookie Hornish and lady driver Fisher run out in front of the pack pleased fans and press alike. In Hornish, Fisher and

Dayton Indy Lights Champion Airton Dare, the series has a trio of potential stars who could become solid gate attractions.

Indy Racing Northern Light Series Race 9
Excite 500
Texas Motor Speedway
October 15, 2000

SCOTT GOODYEAR EXCELS IN THE EXCITE 500. BUDDY LAZIER NOTCHES IRNLS CHAMPIONSHIP

Having announced his retirement, Scott Goodyear ended his season in style, winning the Excite 500 and earning a firm 2001 ride offer from runner-up Eddie Cheever. Buddy Lazier had the second biggest day of his racing career taking down his first IRNLS Championship. He rates his 1996 Indianapolis 500 win as the crowning achievement of his career to date. What he really wants is to win both in the same year. Lazier finished fourth today behind third place Billy Boat who carved his way to the podium from a 22nd starting slot. Eliseo Salazar claimed the final spot in the top five. Airton Dare was running up front with a shot at the win when he ran out of fuel. He settled for Rookie of the Year honors. Lazier's long term car owner Ron Hemelgarn has been an Indy Racing League stalwart from the start and a strong believer in Tony George's formula.

2000 INDY RACING NORTHERN LIGHT SERIES TOP 10 DRIVER EARNINGS	
JUAN MONTOYA	$1,235,690
BUDDY LAZIER	1,168,700
SCOTT GOODYEAR	884,900
EDDIE CHEEVER	876,200
GREG RAY	821,700
ELISEO SALAZAR	820,000
SCOTT SHARP	767,050
AL UNSER JR.	730,300
MARK DISMORE	712,950
ROBBIE BUHL	685,500

Cheryl Day Anderson

Sophomore **SARAH FISHER** proved that she could run with the big boys by placing third at Kentrucky after leading the race for nine laps.

Grand American Road Racing Association

James Weaver Takes the Driver's Championship in a Solid Inaugural Season

The new Grand American Road Racing Association had some big league backers in the France brothers, Bill and Jim of NASCAR fame and a stellar opening act in the Rolex 24 at Daytona, America's premier endurance classic. After nine events, a respectable number for a new series, they also had a deserving champion, James Weaver, by any measure one of the world's elite road racers. Grand Am also had two new classes alongside the familiar divisions for top level prototypes (SportsRacer in the Grand Am designation) and two sizes of Grand Am Touring cars (GTO and GTU). The new divisions were Sports Racer II for smaller displacement V6 powered prototypes and American GT for tube-framed racers similar to Trans-Am cars. True to its NASCAR roots, Grand Am adopted a policy of fine tuning the regulations to promote close racing, rather than yielding center stage to technical standouts.

The new series' inaugural event, and its crown jewel, the Rolex 24 at Daytona, witnessed a huge entry and a Rob Dyson R&S Ford on the pole for the second straight year. James Weaver piloted the car and captained the driving team that put it in the lead by six laps in the 19th hour. At that point, the engine turned sour and two GT cars whistled by, a factory Dodge Viper ably handled by the French Oreca team and a factory Chevrolet Corvette C5R with an all-American driver line up. The Dodge Viper would score the distinctive first ever win in the Rolex 24 for an American GT car,

though a Ford Mustang had come close in an earlier year. The Corvette camp vowed to come back in 2001 and reverse the order. The Dyson car, do-driven by owner Rob Dyson, Max Papis and Elliott Forbes-Robinson as well as Weaver, survived long enough to win the SportsRacer class. Weaver went on to claim four additional poles and four more victories en route to the driver's title with a clear 29 point margin in the final standings. His chief opposition came from Didier Theys in the Judd V10 powered Ferrari 333SP. He won twice in the hybrid, partnered by Freddy Lienhard and Mauro Baldi. For the first time since its arrival on the U.S. endurance racing scene in 1994, a full blooded Ferrari failed to win a race in the series since the factory refused to develop the engine. Most owners gave up on the marque. James Baldwin, the third placed SportsRacer driver in the series, piloted another hybrid, the R&S Judd shared with Irv Hoerr. They, too, won twice. An intriguing pair of Lolas made quite a splash in the series without a trip to victory lane. The Jon Field-Olivier Gavin Lola Ford came close at Watkins Glen but problems in the pits cancelled their chances at top honors. A similar car entered by Phil Creighton attracted attention but was never a factor.

The new SportsRacer II category was dominated by the new Lola Nissan of Larry Merto and Ryan Hampton. They took eight poles and six wins to tie for the driver's title. Next best was the Kudzu Mazda of Richard Grupp and Dennis Spencer, which

won at Watkins Glen. While the Kudzu did not quite fit the category, it was allowed a dispensation and its drivers tied for third in the class championship.

The GTO class was a benefit for the Saleen SR team of Ron Johnson and Terry Borcheller. They passed on the season opener Rolex 24 at Daytona but won eight of the nine events remaining, for a shared runaway victory in the driver's championship. Aside from the Rolex 24 winning Oreca Viper, only the Porsche 911 Turbo driven by David Lacey and Greg Wilkins interrupted the Saleens' winning streak.

The GTU championship was again a Porsche-BMW battleground. Porsche proponents Mike Fitzgerald and Darren Law were the dominant duo with five victories. The driver's title went to Fitzgerald on the basis of points earned in the season opener with a different team. BMW's Rich Fairbanks won three times, twice with Bill Auberlen and once with Andy Pilgrim but finished fifth in the title chase behind Kevin Buckler and Phillip Coltin.

The American GT category, which had plentiful starters but not too many finishers in the longer endurance races, made Doug Mills its first champion. He was followed by the pair of Craig Conway and Doug Goad. For 2001 a slight schedule change and a Rolex 24 at Daytona bolstered by the addition of Dale Earnhardt Jr. and Sr. as Corvette drivers adds momentum to the series as does the addition of Rolex as the title sponsor.

Dan Bianchi

1 Again the class of the field, JAMES WEAVER won five times in the Dyson R&S Ford to take the first ever Grand American Road Racing Driver's Championship in the top SportsRacer class. (334 Grand Am Road Racing points)

Dan Bianchi

2 Extracting the best from the Judd powered Ferrari, **DIDIER THEYS** won twice and proved a gallant runner-up in the new championship. (304 Grand Am Road Racing points)

Dan Bianchi

3 A Judd V10 in an R&S chassis powered **JACK BALDWIN** (shown here with co-driver George Robinson, left) to third place honors on the basis of a pair of victories. (301 Grand Am Road Racing points)

Dan Bianchi

4 DOMENICO SCHIATTARELLA did his best to uphold Ferrari's honor in the 333SP but failed to win a race. (285 Grand Am Road Racing points)

Dan Bianchi

5 Tied for the lead in a shortened '99 season, ELLIOTT FORBES-ROBINSON, of the dominant Dyson Racing team, settled for fifth place in 2000. (263 Grand Am Road Racing points)

LARRY OBERTO, the SportsRacer II Co-Champion tied with partner Ryan Hampton, 274 points.

TERRY BORCHELLER, the GTO Co-Champion tied with partner Ron Johnson, 307 points.

MIKE FITZGERALD, the GTU Champion, 320 points.

DOUG MILLS, the American GT Champion, 320 points.

Grand American Road Racing Race 1
Rolex 24 at Daytona
Daytona International Speedway
February 5-6, 2000

A STUNNING VICTORY FOR THE DODGE VIPER AS GT CARS OUTPACE THE PROTOTYPES

It looked like a clear cut victory for one of Rob Dyson's thundering R&S Fords, sporting a six lap lead after 19 hours. James Weaver had put the car on the pole and captained the driving team that put it in the lead after eight hours and built up the six lap cushion over the next 11 hours. However, lurking in second place was a fast, consistent Dodge Viper GTS-R with a French driving team captained by Olivier Beretta of factory backed Team Oreca. At this point the R&S Ford's engine went off song and the Viper whittled away at the lead. With two hours to go Weaver's lead was down to zero. The Viper slipped past, closely pursued by an arch rival Corvette C5R with lead driver Ron Fellows. This left the struggling but class winning Dyson car in fourth place overall at the end but still 80 laps ahead of the next SportsRacers, a pair of Cadillac LMPs. One of the Cadillacs, with lead driver Wayne Taylor, had led for two hours in the first third of the race.

The Viper victory was the first ever in the classic for an American GT car, although Mustangs entered by Jack Roush had finished second and third overall in two separate editions of the race. The Corvette finished second overall, a mere 31 seconds behind the Viper for the closest finish in Rolex 24 Hours at Daytona history. Third overall went to another Team Oreca car, as did fifth overall. Privateer Vipers filled the sixth and seventh positions. The first GTU entry to finish was the Haberthur Racing Porsche GT3R. The only American GT car to distinguish itself was the 27th overall Comer Racing Chevrolet Camaro. It was 149 laps ahead of the second car in the class, another Camaro, entered by the Spirit of Daytona. The sole Ferrari 333SP, a fierce competitor and former winner in previous Rolex 24s, lasted only 132 laps. With almost 100 entries and a surprise finish, the first Rolex 24 at Daytona under the Grand Am banner was a successful start to what could be an interesting new season.

Grand American Road Racing Race 2
Sun Automotive 200
Phoenix International Raceway
April 22, 2000

IRV HOERR AND JACK BALDWIN IN THEIR NEW LOLA PREVAIL AT PHOENIX ON FUEL STRATEGY

The Judd V10 gets better fuel economy than its SportsRacer competition and the driving pair of Irv Hoerr and Jack Baldwin stretched it further with a short shifting technique. Net result, they, unlike most of the SportsRacers, got away with a single pit stop over 200 miles and earned top honors at Phoenix. Unbelievably, they were on a borrowed engine with 1300 racing miles on the clock. Even then, it took a cut tire on the Andy Wallace-James Weaver R&S Ford, which was leading near the end, to get them into victory lane. Ralf Kelleners, in a Ferrari 330SP, slipped into second place on the Wallace stop, leaving the Dyson drivers Wallace and Weaver with a consolation third place. Fourth went to a Ferrari Judd driven by Freddy Lienhard and Didier Theys. GTO was a romp for Terry Borcheller and Ron Johnson in their new Mustang-based Saleen. BMW fought back from Rolex 24 at Daytona frustrations to take GTU honors with Bill Auberlen and Rick Fairbanks at the wheel of an M3. The Spirit of Daytona Camaro wheeled by Craig Conway and Doug Goad also rebounded to win the American GT class. The new SportsRacer II category for six cylinder cars attracted three entries. The class win went to the Magnum Chevrolet of Ryan Hampton and Larry Oberto who are expected to run a new Lola the rest of the season. Of the 23 starters all but one was running at the finish.

Grand American Road Racing Race 3
Nextel 250
Homestead-Miami Speedway
May 7, 2000

MAURO BALDI AND DIDIER THEYS HOME IN ON THE HOMESTEAD VICTORY

It's owners call it the Doran Special. It's really a Ferrari 333SP into which a V10 Judd engine has been transplanted for more power and better fuel economy. By any name it was the class of the Nextel 250 field. In the hands of Mauro Baldi and Didier Theys it finished a lap ahead of the second place Jack Baldwin-Irv Hoerr R&S Judd. The John Paul Jr.-James Weaver R&S Ford which had been close until its gearbox, like that on the other team car driven by David Bernard and Elliott Forbes-Robinson, folded, salvaged third place overall.

Ryan Hampton and Larry Oberto claimed the SR II honors in their new Lola Nissan, one of three in the event. GTO was again no contest for Terry Borcheller and Ron Johnson in the Mustang-based Saleen. There was, however, plenty of competition in the GTU arena. The Mike Fitzgerald-Darren Law Porsche GT3R proved to be the best of a gaggle of similar machines. The hammer and tongs American GT category was decided by a bumping incident in which the Michael Cohen-Jon Leavy Camaro bested the Craig Conway-Doug Goad Camaro. By any measure it was a lucky day for winners Baldi and Theys. Before borrowing the winning engine they blew two of their own in the race's preliminaries and both of the formidable Dyson cars lost gearboxes, one early, one late

Richard Dole

Dodge Viper GTS-R, outright winner of the Rolex 24 at Daytona and the first American GT car to take top honors in the endurance classic.

Grand American Road Racing Race 4
Dodge Dealers Grand Prix
Lime Rock Park
May 29, 2000

DYSON RACING DOMINATES AT LIME ROCK

James Weaver put Dyson Racing's R&S Ford MKIII on the pole, then he and co-driver Butch Leitzinger put the rest of the field down at least one lap in winning Grand Am's round four at Lime Rock, the team's home track. Freddy Lienhard and Didier Theys, the Homestead winners, finished second in their Doran Special, a lap ahead of the third place Ralf Kelleners-Mimmo Schiattarella Ferrari 333SP. Ryan Hampton and Larry Oberto, in their Lola Nissan were again the class of a small SportsRacer II contingent. At Lime Rock the SportsRacers had their own event leaving the GT cars to run separately.

In the GT only competition the Terry Borcheller-Ron Johnson Saleen was again running away from its competition building up a two lap lead when it made a routine pit stop. Spilled fuel started a fire, which though quickly extinguished, allowed the lead to go up in smoke. Not to worry, Johnson quickly regained the spot to win by 23.384 seconds.

Second overall was the GTU class winning BMW-M3 of Mike Fitzgerald and Darren Law which humbled a five car train of Porsches. The Spirit of Daytona Camaro of Craig Conway and Doug Goad won its second race of the year, compiling a .500 winning average in the American GT class.

The Grand Am philosophy is to keep costs down and the competition level up. In the tube frame, big V8 American GT class, Grand Am has created a category with the lowest costs in major league road racing. While the low budget American GT cars often fail to shine in the longer events such as the Rolex 24 at Daytona, they can compete respectably in the shorter outings.

Grand American Road Racing Race 5
U.S. Road Racing Classic
Mid-Ohio Sports Car Course
June 4, 2000

JACK BALDWIN BLASTS TO MID-OHIO VICTORY

Jack Baldwin played the traffic just right in his R&S Judd to slide past race leader Elliott Forbes-Robinson's R&S Ford and snatch the victory at Mid-Ohio. Forbes-Robinson and co-driver John Paul Jr. had to settle for second place. Forbes-Robinson's teammate James Weaver, along with Butch Leitzinger, had a comfortable lead in the other Dyson R&S Ford when a bolt in the rear suspension broke, necessitating an emergency pit stop, which resulted in a ninth place finish. Scott Schubot and Andy Wallace took third place in their Lola Ford. Larry Oberto and Ryan Hampton made it four in a row for SportsRacer II honors. The news in GTO was that Terry Borcheller and Ron Johnson didn't win in their Saleen. Porsche enthusiasts Greg Wilkins and David Lacey did in an upset. BMW protagonists Mike Fitzgerald and Darren Law made it two in a row over a flock of Porsches.

Camaro mounted Craig Conway and Doug Goad were again the class of the American GT contingent. It was the second victory of the year for overall winner Jack Baldwin, the first for co-driver George Robinson. Seemingly the Dyson R&S Fords enter every event as the favorites but competition is close enough that any slip or slight malfunction can cost them the victory. Certainly in Weaver and Leitzinger, Dyson has two of the quickest drivers on the circuit with Weaver particularly adept in the wet.

Grand American Road Racing Race 6
Paul Revere 250
Daytona International Speedway
June 29, 2000

DYSON RACING'S JAMES WEAVER AND ANDY WALLACE SHINE IN DAYTONA'S NIGHT RACE

For the first time this year a true Ferrari was on the pole in Daytona's nighttime Paul Revere 250. But the best the Italian thoroughbred driven by Ralf Kelleners and Mimmo Schiattarella could do at the end was third place. American muscle in the form of the R&S Ford MKIII prevailed, albeit driven by a pair of Britishers Andy Wallace and James Weaver. The Doran Special, a Ferrari with Judd power, gained runner-up honors with Ross Bentley and Didier Theys at the wheel. Twenty-two SportsRacers including eight in the SRII category started. Ryan Hampton and Larry Oberto in a Lola Nissan again took top honors in this category which has gained support as the season progresses. The normally untouchable Saleen of Terry Borcheller and Ron Johnson proved fragile this time out allowing the Dodge Viper of Marty Miller and Eric Messley to take GTO category honors. Mike Fitzgerald and Darren Law were the class of a fleet of Porsches in GTU while Craig Conway and Doug Goad notched another win in the American GT class. As an interesting sidelight, Jon Field drove all the way in his Lola Ford finishing fifth overall and risking disqualification since the regulations call for two drivers.

One of the Dyson Ford R&S MKIIIs
that carried James Weaver to the
driver's championship.

The Chevrolet Corvette C-5R that finished the Rolex 24 at Daytona a scant 30 seconds behind the winning Viper, in second place overall. It was the closest finish in the race's history.

Grand American Road Racing Race 7
Sargento Road America 500
Elkhart Lake, WI
July 9, 2000

DORAN SPECIAL SCORES AGAIN AT ROAD AMERICA

The combination of Ferrari road holding and Judd power proved unbeatable for the second time this year as the Doran Special handled by Mauro Baldi, Didier Theys and Freddy Lienhard scored the victory.

Again one of the potent Dyson R&S Fords faltered while in the lead. The Andy Wallace-James Weaver car lost two laps to brake problems but still managed to finish fourth ahead of the other team car driven by owner Rob Dyson, John Paul Jr. and Elliott Forbes-Robinson. The all Ferrari 333SP wheeled by Eric van de Poele and Mimmo Schiattarella was the only other car in the field not lapped.

Martin Snow and Larry Schumacher, in a Lola Nissan, took their first SportsRacer II honors of the year. Terry Borcheller and Ron Johnson were back on form and dom-inating the GTO field despite a variety of mechanical problems. A GTU Porsche GT3 driven by Mike Fitzgerald and Darren Law not only took class honors, it was the first GT car to finish. Irv Hoerr, a winner earlier in the year in the SportsRacer class, added American GT honors to his logbook in a Camaro co-driven by Roger Schramm and Werner Frank. In the SportsRacer driver's championship the top five after today's race were: James Weaver, 229; Didier Theys, 216; Jack Baldwin, 215; Elliott Forbes-Robinson, 208 and Mimmo Schiattarella, 206.

Grand American Road Racing Race 8
Players Grand Prix of Trois-Rivieres
Trois-Rivieres, Canada
July 30, 2000

DYSON DUO OF JAMES WEAVER AND BUTCH LEITZINGER TAKES TROIS-RIVIERES HONORS

Ross Bentley and pole winner Didier Theys made it close in their Doran Special, but in the end Dyson's James Weaver and Butch Leitzinger had the upper hand in their R&S Ford MKIII at Trois-Rivieres. The two cars had rotated in the lead on pit stops but on the final countdown American horsepower prevailed, John Paul Jr. and Elliott Forbes-Robinson in a second Dyson entry finished third. Ryan Hampton and Larry Oberto chalked up one more SRII win in their Lola Nissan. Terry Borcheller and Ron Johnson were back on top of the GTO ranks in their Saleen. In GTU, the BMW-M3 of Andy Pilgrim and Rick Fairbanks smartly defeated a much larger Porsche contingent. Camaro drivers Craig Conway and Doug Goad continued their winning ways in their trusty Camaro. It was their fifth American GT win in the year's eight events to date.

Grand American Road Racing Race 9
Bosch Sports Car Summerfest
Watkins Glen, NY
August 27, 2000

DYSON TRIO ON TOP AT WATKINS GLEN

Jon Field and Olivier Gavin, in their Lola Ford, fought the good fight with pole winenr James Weaver and his teammates Butch Leitzinger and Andy Wallace in the Dyson R&S Ford, exchanging the lead five times over the course of 564 miles on the challenging Watkins Glen circuit. However, the Dyson Team was on top in the last exchange and ran off the last 25 laps in the lead, to win by 6.648 seconds. Third place Jack Baldwin and George Robinson, in the R&S MKIII Judd had the only other car on the lead lap.

The first GT car to finish was the GTU Porsche GT3R drvien by Mike Fitzgerald and Darren Law to sixth place overall. Terry Borcheller and Ron Johnson salvaged GTO honors in their Saleen in seventh overall. A surprising 11th overall was the top American GT car, the Camaro driven by Craig Conway and Doug Goad. Ninth overall and first in SportsRacer II went to the Kudzu Mazda of Richard Grupp, Dennis Spencer and Ralph Thomas after the front running Ryan Hampton - Larry Oberto Lola Nissan faltered. A big field of 52 cars started. Weaver's win made him the first ever Grand American Road Racing Association champion.

Richard Dole

Audi R8s won nine of the year's 12 events, six of these in the hands of Allan McNish and Rinaldo Capello.

Professional Sports Car Racing

The American Le Mans Series Expands Overseas as Allan McNish and Audi Claim Championships.

The McNish - Capello Pair Captured Six of the Season's 12 Races, Started on the Pole Eight Times

Only his Audi R8 co-driver Rinaldo Capello came close to new ALMS champion driver Allan McNish and no other manufacturer was truly in the hunt for Audi's runaway manufacturer's title. The co-drivers of the second Audi team car, Emanuele Pirro and Frank Biela, placed third and fourth in the driver's championship. They combined for three wins and notched two poles. Jörg Müller and J.J. Lehto, driving a BMW V12LMR, similar to the one that was so successful in 1999, could only come up with fifth and sixth in the drivers' chase. They won twice and scored a single pole. The leading Panoz drivers, David Brabham and Jan Magnussen, had to settle for seventh and eighth place for the season. Although equally in contention they won only a single race. All three manufacturers fielded spectacular prototypes that indulged in some close battles, but the clear superiority of the Audi squadron emerged as the season progressed; nine wins to two for BMW, one for Panoz. Mimmo Schiattarella drove the Rafanelli Lola Judd to the Silverstone pole to no avail in the race and the gallant privateer was simply outgunned by the well financed factory teams.

In the big GTS division the French Oreca team, driving American Dodge Vipers, again swept away the opposition. Team leader Olivier Beretta was the repeat driver's champion, teammate Karl Wendlinger a close runner-up. The second pair of factory Viper drivers, Tommy Archer and David Donohue checked in third and fourth on the season's leader board. Sixth place Andy Pilgrim was the leading Corvette driver. Chevrolet won twice, in a limited schedule, with all the rest of the events going to Chrysler. However, Porsche gained second place in the Manufacturer's Championship, well behind Chrysler.

In GT, if you weren't driving a Porsche GT3R, you weren't going to make the top of the year's leader board. Dirk Müller, Lucas Luhr, Sascha Maassen, and Bob Wollek, Porsche protagonists, all made it interesting for each other while besting the BMW contingent. They finished the year in that order. Porsche handily took the GT manufacturer's honors over arch rival BMW with 10 victories to just two for BMW.

2001 prototype drivers won't have to worry about McNish. He's off to Formula One as Toyota's test driver. Audi will be back with an updated version of its R8 to fight off the challenge of a team of new Panoz roadsters, designed to wipe away the disappointments of the 2000 season. Indy car driver Gualter Salles has been signed for the Panoz driving team. With Team Oreca bowing out of the American Le Mans Series for a new Chrysler assignment at the prototype level, two of their all conquering Vipers of 2000 will be campaigned in 2001 by the new American Viper Team. Also new for the upcoming season will be Champion Racing's entry of an Audi R8, the first ever in private hands.

Of particular interest in 2001 will be the debut of the new LMP 675 class for prototypes with V8 engines up to 3.5 liters. One of the first entries will be Knight Racing's Lola Judd. A new event at Texas Motor Speedway opens ALMS' 2001 season.

MANUFACTURER'S CHAMPIONSHIP

PROTOTYPES:	GTS:	GT:
AUDI 264	DAIMLERCHRYSLER 266	PORSCHE 270
BMW 217	PORSCHE 199	BMW 202
PANOZ 208	CHEVROLET 136	

Richard Dole

1 ALLAN McNISH captained an all-star driving team in the all conquering Audi R8 factory team and earned the Driver's Championship in the prcoess. He's off to Formula One in 2001 as Toyota's test driver. (270 points)

Richard Dole

2 McNish's highly capable co-driver **RINALDO CAPELLO** was the deserving runner-up in the Driver's Championship. He's likely to be nominated for the lead role in Audi's 2001 campaign in the American Le Mans Series. (257 points)

Richard Dole

3 The second factory Audi R8 had **EMANUELE PIRRO** as its top pilot. He scored the year's third highest point total. (232 points)

Richard Dole

4 FRANK BIELA, Pirro's co-driver, landed in fourth place on the year's leader board. (231 points)

Richard Dole

5 Gallant effort by BMW LMRV12 driver JÖRG MÜLLER netted a pair of vitories but only fifth place behind the Audi quartet. (221 points)

Richard Dole

1 Captain of the dominant Viper mounted Team Oreca, **OLIVIER BERETTA** easily out-distanced the opposition for the GTS Championship. (268 points)

Richard Dole

1 Outpacing a squadron of fellow Porsche GT3R drivers **DIRK MÜLLER** made it to the top of the GT contingent. (223 points)

Ken Hawking

The gallant effort of J.J. Lehto and Jörg Müller in one of the BMW LMRV12s couldn't stem the Audi avalanche but they scored a pair of victories.

American Le Mans Series Race 1
Superflo 12 Hours at Sebring
Sebring International Raceway
March 18, 2000

SEBRING FALLS TO AUDI ASSAULT

A pair of gleaming silver Audi R8s swept the 48th running of the Superflo 12 Hours at Sebring, America's oldest sportscar race. Pole winner Frank Biela led the winning driving team, which included regular partners Emanuele Pirro and Tom Kristensen. After 12 hours of racing on the refurbished airport circuit before a race day crowd in excess of 80,000, they were 39.111 seconds ahead of a sister R8, handled by Rinaldo capello, Allan McNish and Michele Alboreto. Both Audis were up a lap on the third place BMW V12LMR, chauffeured by J.J. Lehto and Jörg Müller which, in turn, was a lap up on its sister BMW with Bill Auberlen, Steve Soper and Jean-Marc Gounon behind the wheel. The Cadillac Northstar LMP of Wayne Taylor and Eric van de Poele, finished sixth, the best of three entered.

In short, it was a clear demonstration of the power of the factory teams. Ironically, the only factory team not to make the race's top 10 was the Panoz pair entered by series founder and Sebring race promoter Don Panoz. The David Brabham, Jan Magnussen Panoz Roadster S forged into the lead twice mid-race but expired with engine problems after 249 laps. The Johnny O'Connell - Hiroki Katoh team car was sidelined after 79 laps with mechanical bothers.

GTS was a runaway for the three Team Oreca Vipers which took all three top places in the category, with Olivier Beretta and Karl Wendlinger leading the charge in seventh place overall.

GT was a Porsche parade with Dirk Müller and Lucas Luhr out in front as the class winners. An outstanding field of 42 cars took the starter's flag.

American Le Mans Series Race 2
Grand Prix of Charlotte
Lowe's Motor Speedway
April 1, 2000

BMW'S JÖRG MÜLLER & J.J. LEHTO CAPTURE CHARLOTTE VICTORY

CART veteran J.J. Lehto put the BMW LMR on the pole at Charlotte, was soon passed by Panoz Roadster S pilot Jan Magnussen but Lehto co-driver Jörg Müller pulled out the victory with his final stint at the wheel. In between, the BMW and the Panoz, co-driven by David Brabham, put on a crowd pleasing battle with five lead changes over the two hour 45 minute encounter on Charlotte's road circuit. Mimmo Schiattarella and Didier de Radigues claimed third place in their Lola Judd ahead of the second BMW. The Audi R8s had a disappointing outing. The top entry finished sixth in the hands of Emanuele Pirro and Frank Biela. The second, driven by Allan McNish and Rinaldo Capello completed only 93 laps. A Team Oreca Viper, with Karl Wendlinger and Olivier Beretta in charge, posted its seventh straight ALMS win in the big GTS class. Porsche drivers Vic Rice and Zak Brown were second in the class, down five laps to the leading Viper. A great drive netted Porsche GT3R pilot Sascha Maassen and Brian Cunningham the GT win over the Cunningham brothers' BMW M3 and a handsome ninth overall. Twenty-one cars were running at the finish, with only two sidelined due to accident or mechanical failure, making the event a clean, exciting display of top flight sports car machinery and driving talent. After their convincing one-two victory from the pole in the opening Sebring round, the lackluster performance of the Audi factory cars today was a bit of a mystery to trackside observers. The Audi effort is a very serious, well planned endeavor and even one race departure from contender status is not in their game plan.

American Le Mans Series Race 3
Silverstone 500, USA Challenge
Silverstone Circuit Ltd., England
May 13, 2000

LEHTO & MÜLLER SCORE TWO IN A ROW FOR BMW AT SILVERSTONE

For the second race in a row Jörg Müller mounted a late race rush, brought victory to the BMW camp. Teammate J.J. Lehto provided generous assistance. Chief opposition came from the Panoz Roadster S handled by Jan Magnussen and David Brabham which checked in with runner-up honors. The Panoz pair might have won except for a failed one stop fuel strategy. Allan McNish put the Audi R8 into the mid-race lead before fading to third at the end with a deflating tire. The pole winning Lola Judd of Mimmo Schiattarella and Didier de Radigues suffered a broken throttle cable early and never recovered from the time lost to repairs. The two Oreca Vipers again dismissed their opposition, with the GTS class winning Beretta - Wendlinger car finishing eighth overall and lapping the sister Donohue - Archer machine. Bob Wollek and Sascha Maassen again bested a group of five Porsche GT3Rs as well as a pair of BMW-M3s for top GT honors, turning on headlights and adding an endurance flavor to the three hour event. Quite a few of the teams involved viewed the Silverstone round as a warm-up for next month's Le Mans 24 Hours, the world's premiere endurance event and the one that manufacturers most want to win. The BMW forces could take encouragement from today's result while the Audi team may want to do a little fine tuning. Although disappointed in missing the victory today, the Panoz forces took consolation in a close second place and the knowledge that a better fuel strategy could have made the difference. The GTS class Vipers came away exuding confidence and Porsche's strong privateer army appeared to be the class of the GT class.

Founder Don Panoz saw his American Le Mans Series through a strong sophomore season and his Panoz LMP prototypes prevail against the factory Audi and BMW efforts at Nurburgring.

American Le Mans Series Race 4
Bitburger/AvD 1000 km
Nurburgring, Germany
July 9, 2000

JAN MAGNUSSEN & DAVID BRABHAM TAKE THE VICTORY FOR PANOZ AT NURBURGRING

Panoz pilot Jan Magnussen snatched the Nurburgring lead from pole winner Rinaldo Capello in the Lola Judd on the first lap and gave it up only on pit stops. He was a clear one minute, 33.627 seconds ahead of the runner-up BMW V12LMR chauffeured by J.J. Lehto and Jörg Müller at the end of the race's 185 laps totalling 523.727 miles. Lehto and Müller, winners at Charlotte and Silverstone, survived a late race spin in taking runner-up honors. Frank Biela and Emanuele Pirro in the best of the Audi R8s had to settle for third place. Alternating rain and dry conditions made the driving tricky and only the truly focused drivers escaped without a spin.

The winning GTS class Viper of Olivier Beretta and Karl Wendlinger spun more than once but still finished 14 laps ahead of the second place Viper, a private entry handled by Steve Watson and Zavier Pompidou. For a change Sascha Maassen and Bob Wollek didn't win the GT category. A suspected oil leak felled them while in the lead leaving top honors in the group to Dirk Müller and Lucas Luhr, driving the obligatory Porsche GT3R. The ALMS driving fraternity thoroughly enjoyed their visit to the fabled Nurburgring and hope to return in 2001. With its visits to Silverstone and Nurburgring, the American Le Mans Series has carved out a new dimension for an American based sports car group. A projected year end event in Adelaide, Australia, would carry the concept further. ALMS founder Don Panoz goes beyond his organizational role in the series by entering his own unique front engined Panoz roadsters, one of which captured today's pole and win.

American Le Mans Series Race 5
Grand Prix of Sonoma
Sears Point Raceway
July 23, 2000

IT'S AN ALL AUDI DAY AT SEARS POINT, ALLAN McNISH & RINALDO CAPELLO BEAT TEAM-MATES EMANUELE PIRRO & FRANK BIELA

Allan McNish placed his Audi R8 on the pole and led the first 36 laps. Teammate Rinaldo Capello led the last 36 laps to the checker and the victory in Sears Point's Grand Prix of Sonoma. They lapped the second place sister car handled by Frank Biela and Emanuele Pirro for a convincing Audi win. The second Audi was in turn a lap ahead of the pair of BMW V12LMRs in the third and fourth finishing slots. J.J. Lehto and Jörg Müller piloted the first of the BMWs, Bill Auberlen and Jean-Marc Gounon, the second. The first Panoz Roadster S in the contest came away with fifth place, handled by David Brabham and Jan Magnussen.

The Oreca Vipers once again dominated the GTS group, with the usual team order reversed. David Donohue and Tommy Archer topped Olivier Beretta and Karl Wendlinger this time. GT turned out to be a bit of an upset - until inspectors got busy post-race. Boris Said and Hans Stuck, in the leading BMW-M3, placed 10th overall and beat a gaggle of Porsche GT3Rs. The inspectors found an over-sized fuel tank in the BMW drawing disqualification and handing the win to Lucas Luhr and Dirk Müller, the Porsche stalwarts who edged similarly mounted Sascha Maassen and Bob Wollek. In the top prototype category the wins now stand Audi, 2; BMW, 2 and Panoz, 1. The BMW pair of Jörg Müller and J.J. Lehto still topped the Driver's Championship with Panoz's Jan Magnussen and David Brabham in pursuit. Team Oreca's Viper drivers Olivier Beretta and Karl Wendlinger were out in front for GTS honors.

American Le Mans Series Race 6
Globemegawheels.com Grand Prix
Mosport International Raceway
August 6, 2000

AUDI's ALLAN McNISH & RINALDO CAPELLO EDGE BMW'S JÖRG MÜLLER & BILL AUBERLEN FOR THE MOSPORT VICTORY

Audi's Rinaldo Capello led BMW's Jörg Müller across the finish line at the end of a hotly contested Mosport round by a couple of car lengths, a mere .148 second after two hours and 45 minutes. The race was an up and down affair in track conditions ranging from wet and slick at the outset to dry and fast at the end. Among the top contenders to spin a crash out of contention were the Jan Magnussen - David Brabham Panoz which exited after 40 laps and the Frank Biela - Emanuele Pirro Audi R8 which had started on the pole. They completed 85 laps. At the end, Müller, on fading tires, just failed to run down Capello who had been handed a huge lead by co-driver Allan McNish. The second BMW V12LMR with Bill Auberlen and Jean-Marc Gounon at the controls finished third.

The GTS battle was a crowd pleaser. Canadian driver and local hero Ron Fellows qualified first in the category and with co-driver Andy Pilgrim made a gallant attempt to unseat the dominant Oreca team but fell short by .353 second to the Viper driven by Olivier Beretta and Karl Wendlinger who finished third overall. The GT category honors went, for the first time, to the Randy Pobst - Bruno Lambert Porsche GT3R. They were a lap up on the second place BMW driven by Boris Said and Hans Stuck. Under the guidance of Don Panoz the track has been much improved since 1999. An item duly recognized and appreciated by the ALMS driving fraternity. In 1999, the factory BMW team declined to start at Mosport due to safety considerations. They were out in full force today and, indeed, almost pulled out the victory.

American Le Mans Series Race 7
Grand Prix of Texas
Texas Motor Speedway
September 2, 2000

AUDI MAKES IT THREE IN A ROW AS FRANK BIELA & EMANUELE PIRRO PREVAIL AT TEXAS MOTOR SPEEDWAY

Allan McNish put his Audi R8 on the pole at Texas with a record 114.747 mph lap and he, along with co-driver Rinaldo Capello, led every lap on the fast Texas Motor Speedway circuit until nine laps from the end. At that point they had to dash into the pits for a splash of fuel, handing the win to their team car, driven by Emanuele Pirro and Frank Biela. Both BMWs had a lap on the third place Panoz Roadster S handled by Jan Magnussen and David Brabham. The usually competitive pair of BMW V12LMRs were two laps further in arrears at the end of the two hour, 45 minute contest.

There was big news in the Corvette camp. The lone C5R, driven by Ron Fellows and Andy Pilgrim, had at last bested the powerful Oreca team led by the Olivier Beretta - Karl Wendlinger car which ended up two laps down to the red bowtie brigade. Randy Pobst and Bruno Lambert continued their winning ways taking GT honors in their Porsche GT3R over similarly mounted Dirk Müller and Lucas Luhr. The race was conducted at night at temperatures in the 100° range, imposing an additional hurdle for drivers, some of whom were slowed by dehydration. In the post-race post mortem it turned out that Capello might not have needed to pit for fuel. His radio was malfunctioning and he made the move as a safety measure. Despite the on rushing Audi juggernaut, BMW's Jörg Müller topped the charts for the Driver's Championship with co-driver J.J. Lehto in second place. Viper's Olivier Beretta and Karl Wendlinger had a sizeable bulge over BMW's David Donohue on the GTS ladder.

American Le Mans Series Race 8
Rose City Grand Prix
Portland International Raceway
September 10, 2000

AUDI'S STREAK EXTENDS TO FOUR, AS RINALDO CAPELLO & ALLAN McNISH PREVAIL IN PORTLAND

It was Rinaldo Capello's turn to claim the pole position in his Audi R8 and motor on to victory circle in Portland, as he, along with co-driver Allan McNish, overcame an early race encounter with a GT car to take the top honors and log four wins in a row for Audi. Pitting under yellow to repair the damage, it took the pair 50 laps to get back into the lead. Once in front, nobody challenged, not even the second place sister car handled by Emanuele Pirro and Frank Biela, which ended up fourth at the end. The closest pursuer to the winning Audi was the David Brabham - Jan Magnussen Panoz Roadster S but even the runner-up was a lap down. The top BMW, piloted by J.J. Lehto and Jörg Müller had to settle for third place. The Cadillac Northstar LMP handled by Max Angelelli and Wayne Taylor finished eighth. Team Oreca's Oliver Beretta and Karl Wendlinger were back in form, once again the class of the GTS group, two laps ahead of their second place sister car piloted by Tommy Archer and David Donohue. In between this pair in 11th overall was the GT class winning Porsche GT3R of Sascha Maassen and Bob Wollek ahead of the second in class BMW-M3 driven by Boris Said and Johannes van Overbeek. Despite the string of Audi wins, BMW pilot Jörg Müller retained a tenuous lead in the battle for the 2000 Driver's Championship. With four victories in a row it's becoming very clear that Audi's all out factory effort will not be denied. The technology, the drivers, and the management all are top drawer. Fast in qualifying, fast and consistent in races, it appears to be only a matter of time for one of their drivers to gain the points lead.

American Le Mans Series Race 9
Petit Le Mans
Road Atlanta Motor Sports Center
September 30, 2000

AUDIS FINISH 1-2 AT PETIT LE MANS FOR FIFTH VICTORY IN A ROW

There's nothing "petit" about Petit Le Mans any longer. A record crowd made full use of every vantage point in Don Panoz's beautifully manicured facility and was treated to a full palette of world class endurance racing. The by now familiar faces of Allan McNish and Rinaldo Capello were smiling on the victory podium after their Audi R8 beat the sister car of Emanuele Pirro, the second fastest qualifier, and Frank Biela by three full laps after a little more than nine hours of racing that covered just over one thousand miles. The second Audi had its hands full with the third place Panoz of David Brabham and Jan Magnussen who were only half a second behind. Corvette co-pilots Andy Pilgrim and Kelly Collins pulled off the GTS win against the favored Oreca Viper Team for their second victory of the year. The leading Viper today, second in class, was handled by Tommy Archer and Patrick Huisman. Oreca team captain Olivier Beretta and Karl Wendlinger finished fourth behind another Corvette with Ron Fellows and Chris Kneifel at the wheel. In a spectacular accident Bill Auberlen's BMW did a complete back flip on the main straight before landing on its wheels. He walked away with a bruised shoulder. Another accident victim was Porsche GT3R driver Paul Newman who lost an encounter with Oliver Gavin's Lola Judd. Newman's car clouted a retaining wall but he walked away uninjured. The race attracted 39 starters and is rapidly becoming a world class endurance classic. Drivers and spectators alike applaud the circuit's amenities, which include the nearby Chateau Élan and Winery, a world class hostelry with full sports facilities.

American Le Mans Series Race 10
Global Center Sports Car Championships
Laguna Seca Raceway
October 15, 2000

FIFTH WIN OF THE YEAR FOR THE AUDI PAIR OF McNISH AND CAPELLO AT LAGUNA SECA

Pole winner Rinaldo Capello set a new record in qualifying but he and partner Allan McNish needed a lot of hustle to win the Laguna Seca round. An early spin dropped them to fifth and the race looked to be the property of the leading Panoz of Jan Magnussen and David Brabham which had qualified on the front row and motored off to a sizeable lead. However, after leading laps 40 through 52 the Panoz engine went off song and finally quit after completing 66 laps, just short of midway. this bit of misfortune for the Panoz handed the lead to the other Audi, handled by Frank Biela and Emanuele Pirro. With 36 laps to go McNish cleanly disposed of the Biela - Pirro team car and closed out the race for a one-two Audi finish. A pair of BMW LMRV12s followed in third and fourth place, the Jörg Müller - J.J. Lehto car leading that of Bill Auberlen and Jean-Marc Gounon.

The GTS contingent found the Olivier Beretta - Karl Wendlinger Viper in the winner's circle, followed by the Andy Pilgrim - Ron Fellow Corvette, and the second Oreca Viper. BMW pilots Hans Stuck and Boris Said combined to thwart a large field of Porsche GT3Rs, best of which was that driven by Randy Pobst and Bruno Lambert. An imposing field of 13 prototypes started. Indy car driver Stefan Johansson teamed with Guy Smith to bring their Reynard Judd home fifth, ahead of Jon Field and Rick Sutherland in their Lola Judd. The factory Cadillac Northstar checked in seventh, driven by Wayne Taylor and Max Angelelli, on the same lap as the leading Viper. Franz Konrad and Charlie Slater drove a Lola Ford to 12th overall.

American Le Mans Series Race 11
Grand Prix of Las Vegas
Las Vegas Motor Speedway
October 9, 2000

AUDIS LAP THE LAS VEGAS FIELD WITH FRANK BIELA AND EMANUELE PIRRO SCORING THE VICTORY

Emanuele Pirro needed a bit of gambler's luck to score the Las Vegas victory for Audi and teammate Frank Biela. With 45 minutes to go in the two hour, 45 minute contest Pirro was riding in fourth place with little prospect of turning it into first place. At that point the lead BMW with Jörg Müller at the wheel appeared to be in command. However, Müller tangled with a lapped car and was, in turn, bumped by Rinaldo Capello's second place Audi. Third place David Brabham in a Panoz got caught up in the encounter and spun in turn. In the space of a few seconds, fourth place Pirro was now the leader, a position he held for 46 laps to the finish. Capello recovered for a second place finish, Müller did not, exiting after 106 laps. The second BMW of Bill Auberlen and Jean-Marc Gounon also benefitted from the tangle, picking up third place.

The familiar names of Olivier Beretta and Karl Wendlinger topped the GTS class over Oreca Viper teammates Tommy Archer and David Donohue. Bob Wollek and Sascha Maassen were again the GT class winners over Lucas Luhr and Dirk Müller, both teams aboard Porsche GT3Rs. While the overall Driver's Championship is still unsettled going into Adelaide's final round, the odds favored Allan McNish. Five records were set over the weekend: Allan McNish's 121.571 mph in prototype qualifying was the first. Lucas Luhr set a new GT qualifying mark at 104.052 mph. During the race, new fastest lap records were set in all three classes. McNish's 118.641 mph set the prototype. Olivier Beretta set the GTS record at 107.656 mph and GT's Dirk Müller set the record at 103.198 mph.

American Le Mans Series Race 12
The Race of a Thousand Years
Adelaide, South Australia
December 31, 2000

ALLAN McNISH & AUDI RUN AWAY WITH THE RACE OF A THOUSAND YEARS

Allan McNish and his Audi R8 romped home 21 laps ahead of the closest opposition in Australia's season ending six hour race. McNish and driving partner Rinaldo Capello didn't even have to contend with the second Audi team car, driven by Emanuele Pirro and Frank Biela. Pirro went off course midrace and damaged his Audi severely. Closest but not very close, opposition came from the runner-up Franz Konrad - Alan Heath - Charlie Slater Lola Ford, which finished on the same lap as the Olivier Beretta - Karl Wendlinger Dodge Viper third overall and again the class of the GTS field. This was the ALMS swan song for the all conquering Oreca team which moves on the prototype scene in 2001. Jean-Philippe Belloc and Ni Amorim, in the second Oreca viper, were fourth overall, second in GTS. Lucas Luhr and Dirk Müller gave their GT3R Porsche a rousing ride for fifth overall, first in the GT group. Christian Menzel, Randy Wars and John Graham were close behind in sixth overall, second best in GT. The three Panoz roadsters expected to give the Audis a tussle for overall honors were all victimized by off-course excursions. So were the pair of Cadillac LMPs which exited early with mechanical problems. His victory fittingly crowned Allan McNish as the ALMS Driver's Champion. He's departing the series on a high note, having been designated the test driver for Toyota's new Formula One team. GTS' repeat champion, Olivier Beretta, will also be moving on. His Oreca team will represent Dodge at the prototype level in 2001. GT champion Dirk Müller was the best of the dominant Porsche drivers.

1 No. 2 no longer **BRIAN SIMO** wrested the Trans-Am driver's title from Paul Gentilozzi. He won three of the year's first four races. (261 BFGoodrich Tires Trans-Am points)

BFGoodrich Tires Trans-Am Series

Runner-Up No Longer, Brian Simo Bests Paul Gentilozzi in the Driver's Championship

At the outset of the 2000 season, two-time champion Paul Gentilozzi had an ambitious game plan; win his third championship in a row with his third different car manufacturer, this time a handsome new Jaguar XKR. Brian Simo's plan was simpler; just win his first championship after three frustrating years as runner-up. He, too, had a new mount, the exotic Qvale Mangusta with sleek Italian coachwork and Ford power.

As the season opened, Simo jumped off to a huge lead. He won three of the first four events including the big Sebring opener. Beset by bad luck, Gentilozzi had nothing higher than a single second place to show for his efforts at this stage. Then his campaign got into gear. Starting with Detroit, "home track" for his sponsor, Johnson Controls HomeLink, he won three in a row and, with two races to go in the 12 race schedule, he enjoyed a 29 point lead over Simo, despite not registering another win after his three race streak. At the penultimate Las Vegas round, Gentilozzi tagged the wall hard enough to put him on the sidelines. Simo didn't have a great day but picked up enough points with a 14th place finish to put a big dent in Gentilozzi's lead. In the San Diego finale pole winner Simo opted for a conservative third place and a sure championship after Gentilozzi went out with a failed oil pump.

Strangely enough, after his big early season surge, Simo never won again. Nor did Gentilozzi after his third race mid-season winning streak. He finished first in Houston but was penalized for a pit violation.

In 1999, all but one race fell to the Gentilozzi - Simo pair. That one went to Chris Neville, who picked up the Houston win when Gentilozzi was pushed back to an official sixth place finish. Neville finished fifth on the year's leader board and will be back in 2001 with higher placement in his sights. After the Simo - Gentilozzi pair, third place for the year went to Jeff Altenburg, a 38 year old rookie. He had a Jaguar XKR, like Gentilozzi's, maintained by Gentilozzi's Rocketsports Racing. In his first race at Sebring he made the podium as he did three more times over the season. No wins came his way but he'll be targeting the top slot in 2001. He was the clear cut winner of the Red Line Oil Rookie of the Year award. Fourth place Leighton Reese won the heat plagued Texas Motor Speedway round, his first ever victory, and the first of the year for Pontiac. He had a clear shot at the Sebring win, but was bunted out of contention on the last lap. Like Altenburg, he'll be back in 2001. Not among the first time winners of 2000 was Tomy Drissi who seemed to have prevailed in the Long Beach round but lost out on a ruling that the race had actually ended one lap earlier and ended the year in sixth place on the leader board.

Veteran Willy T. Ribbs failed to make victory circle but a pair of podium placements helped him into seventh place for the year.

Johnny Miller was the beneficiary of the Long Beach ruling that took the win away from Drissi. He also won a pair of poles but had hoped for a higher year end placement than the eighth he registered. Jack Willes, runner-up to Altenburg in the Rookie of the Year contest, made the podium twice, en route to ninth place in the championship. Simon Gregg completed the year's top 10 on consistency despite a lack of podium placement. Rookie Kenny Wilden was the surprise winner on the challenging Laguna Seca road circuit in only his fifth BF Goodrich Tires Trans-Am outing. He also picked up the Simple Green Clean Up award which had accumulated to $40,000 by the time he won it.

Boris Said, a regular on other circuits but only an occasional Trans-Am pilot, picked up the win at Las Vegas, after placing second in the previous round, both at the wheel of a new Mustang Cobra. Though none of them competed in the entire series three lady drivers livened up the rookie scene Monica Kolvyn, Marybeth Harrison and Linda Pobst. Under relaxed rules for 2000, the two new nameplates, Qvale Mangusta and Jaguar XKR both scored victories as did old standbys Ford Mustang Cobra, Pontiac Grand Prix and Chevrolet's Camaro and Corvette. With fuel injection and overhead cam engines now allowed, there may be more new models in 2001 when the series expects to continue its upward course of 2000.

Dan Bianchi

2 His luck ran out. **PAUL GENTILOZZI,** ahead by 29 points with two races to go, DNF'd in both, missed his goal of three championships in a row in three different car makes. (249 BFGoodrich Tires Trans-Am points)

Dan Bianchi

4 **LEIGHTON REESE** got his first ever Trans-Am victory and enough top five placements to hold fourth place in the title run. (190 BFGoodrich Tires Trans-Am points)

Dan Bianchi

5 **CHRIS NEVILLE** scored his second career Trans-Am victory, with better luck would have had more. He completed the top five. (180 BFGoodrich Tires Trans-Am points)

BFGoodrich Tires Trans-Am Series Race 1
48th Annual Superflo 12 Hours at Sebring
Sebring, FL
March 17, 2000

BRIAN SIMO WINS WILD SEBRING SEASON OPENER

Brian Simo went from last to lead just one lap, the final one, to score the season opening win at Sebring International Raceway. For his new Tommy Bahama Qvale Mangusta it was a debut victory. Chris Neville finished second and rookie Jeff Altenburg made the podium in third place in his first Trans-Am outing. Some luck was required. With two laps remaining, a caution dictated a one lap shootout to the checker. On the green, leader Johnny Miller and Leighton Reese tangled handing the lead to third place Chris Neville. Simo, now in second place, disposed of Neville for the last lap win. Rookie Altenburg, Jaguar XKR mounted, inherited third place. Early in the race reigning champion Paul Gentilozzi sustained a cut tire while in the lead but salvaged fourth place, ahead of Lou Gigliotti.

BFGoodrich Tires Trans-Am Series Race 2
The Grand Prix of Charlotte
Lowe's Motor Speedway
April 1, 2000

BRIAN SIMO MAKES IT TWO FOR TWO WITH CHARLOTTE WIN

Brian Simo won his second race in a row at Lowe's Motor Speedway. Runner-up Paul Gentilozzi once again was a victim of accident debris and the resultant unscheduled pit stop. After the stop he mounted a charge that fell short. Again a rookie took down the third finishing spot, this time Jack Willes. Stu Hayner was a factor until tangling with John Paul Jr. There were three cautions during the race, with Peter Shea, Jeff Altenburg and Michael Lewis numbered among the day's losers. Chris Neville and Tomy Drissi were among those who escaped the encounters. They finished fourth and fifth, respectively. Both events this year have been marked by Simo being on the receiving end of good fortune and arch rival Gentilozzi frantically attempting to make up for bad luck.

BFGoodrich Tires Trans-Am Series Race 3
The Johnson Controls 100
Toyota Grand Prix of Long Beach
April 16, 2000

JOHNNY MILLER SCORES HIS FIRST CAREER VICTORY AT LONG BEACH

Johnny Miller had come close to victory before. Long Beach looked to be another of his near misses. Tomy Drissi was at first declared the winner. Then the stewards decided that the race's 35th lap had occurred after the 60 minute time limit had occurred. Miller was declared the winner with Chris Neville and Tomy Drissi awarded the other two podium finishes. Claudio Burtin and Steve Pelke rounded out the top five. For the third time in the year's three races, Paul Gentilozzi encountered misfortune while leading. There was no recovery this time; a broken valve train ended his day early. Two race winner Brian Simo had his turn to suffer adversity, a cut tire forcing an unwanted pit stop. On the race's 35th lap, which turned out not to count, there was a major multiple car crash, happily resulting in no injuries.

BFGoodrich Tires Trans-Am Series Race 4
Mosport International Raceway
Bowmanville, Ontario, Canada
May 21, 2000

BRIAN SIMO MAKES MOSPORT HIS THIRD WIN OF 2000

1999 champion Paul Gentilozzi suffered more bad luck at Mosport, this time of his own making. On the pole and leading all the way, he spun under pressure from second fastest qualifier Brian Simo who cruised onward to the win. Behind the lead pair Randy Ruhlman and Johnny Miller were hotly contesting the final podium position. This contest ended in spins for both, taking them out of contention. This handed second place honors to Jeff Altenburg and third to Tomy Drissi. Lou Gigliotti notched fourth place, followed by Stu Hayner in fifth. Despite all his misfortune Gentilozzi was riding in second place on the year's leader board with 90 points behind Simo (117) and ahead of Drissi (82), Neville (74) and Gigliotti (69).

BFGoodrich Tires Trans-Am Series Race 5
The Johnson Controls 100
Tenneco Automotive Grand Prix of Detroit
June 17, 2000

PAUL GENTILOZZI WINS DETROIT'S JOHNSON CONTROLS 100

Paul Gentilozzi knows where his sponsor's bread is buttered and when his sponsor is also the race sponsor he puts forth a special effort. The effort paid off in his first victory of the year before a large contingent of automotive industry executives in the crowd. The win was doubly sweet since it was at the expense of arch rival Brian Simo who had to settle for runner-up honors. Veteran Willy T. Ribbs gained his first podium of the year with his third place. Behind the lead pack of Gentilozzi, Simo and Ribbs, there were numerous incidents. G.J. Mennen and Jack Willes managed to avoid them and were rewarded with the remaining spots in the top five. Ribbs' podium placement moved him into the year's top five in points, displacing Chris Neville.

BFGoodrich Tires Trans-Am Series Race 6
Simple Green Trans-Am 100
Burke Lakefront Airport, Cleveland, OH
July 1, 2000

PAUL GENTILOZZI MAKES IT TWO IN A ROW AT CLEVELAND

Paul Gentilozzi continued his winning ways in Cleveland, leading every lap from the pole. Rival Brian Simo made a gallant effort to catch Gentilozzi but, burdened with a last place starting position due to qualifying problems, could only reach third place at the finish. Runner-up Johnny Miller was 1.593 seconds behind at the checker. Jeff Altenburg and Lou Gigliotti completed the top five. With Simo mired so far back in the pack and Miller unable to mount a meaningful challenge, the race was a romp for Gentilozzi who now appears on track in his campaign for a third consecutive title. Though still trailing in the points parade, he is gaining momentum in his effort to dislodge Simo from the leadership position he has enjoyed all year.

BFGoodrich Tires Trans-Am Series Race 7
Motorola 200 CART FedEx Weekend
Elkhart Lake, WI
August 19, 2000

BFGoodrich Tires Trans-Am Series Race 8
Grand Prix of Texas
Texas Motor Speedway
September 3, 2000

BFGoodrich Tires Trans-Am Series Race 9
Texaco-Havoline Grand Prix of Houston
Houston, TX
September 30, 2000

PAUL GENTILOZZI TAKES HIS THIRD WIN IN A ROW AT ROAD AMERICA

LEIGHTON REESE BEATS THE HEAT TO SCORE HIS FIRST EVER VICTORY

CHRIS NEVILLE GETS THE HOUSTON WIN AS GENTILOZZI GETS PENALTY

Not even a major pileup involving Kenny Wilden, Paul Fox and Lou Gigliotti, which halted the race for 20 minutes, could stop Paul Gentilozzi on his course to victory at Elkhart Lake. It was his third in a row and elevated him to first place in the points race over Brian Simo who spun early and finished a lowly 20th, down a lap, and behind lady driver Marybeth Harrison. Second place went to Jeff Altenburg, 5.021 seconds in arrears, for a Jaguar XKR one-two finish. Tony Ave notched the third podium position with fourth going to Leighton Reese and fifth to Michael Lewis. The win put Gentilozzi in the points lead for the first time this year with 192 over Simo (178). As in the past two years' contests, the championship is again shaping up as a Gentilozzi-Simo duel to the finish.

Leighton Reese kept his cool in the 100° heat at Texas Motor Speedway to score his first career BFGoodrich Tires Trans-Am victory. Series leader Paul Gentilozzi and Brian Simo came away a little hot under the collar and pointless for the day. Gentilozzi burned a cylinder. Pole winner Simo suffered a flat tire and subsequent suspension damage. With these front runners out of the way, Reese worked his way up to second place and soon got by new leaders Johnny Miller and Michael Lewis for the win. Miller salvaged runner-up honors, Lewis faded to fifth at the end. Jeff Altenburg and Simon Gregg picked up the third and fourth finishing slots. Reese's win was also the first for Pontiac this year. Gentilozzi continues to lead the driver's championship with 196 points.

Paul Gentilozzi, in the Johnson Controls HomeLink Jaguar XKR, crossed the finish line first in the Houston round despite suffering a cut tire in a bumping duel with arch rival Brian Simo that required a pit stop. The officials ruled that his crew had five men over the pit wall to change the tire and he was dropped to sixth place. Simo, in the Tommy Bahama Qvale Mangusta, ended up fourth. The race win went to Chris Neville and runner-up honors to Stu Hayner with the third podium position falling to G.J. Mennen. Jack Willes, who crossed the finish line in third place, was bumped to ninth for passing under the yellow. Leighton Reese picked up the final top five finish. The penalty to Gentilozzi could prove critical in his close championship race with Simo.

Ken Hawking

Mark Weber

BFGoodrich Tires Trans-Am Series Race 10	BFGoodrich Tires Trans-Am Series Race 11	BFGoodrich Tires Trans-Am Series Race 12
GlobalCenter Sports Car Championships	Johnson Controls 100	San Diego Grand Prix
Monterey, CA	Las Vegas Motor Speedway	San Diego Street Course
October 15, 2000	October 29, 2000	November 5, 2000

KENNY WILDEN WINS HIS FIRST CAREER RACE AT LAGUNA SECA

In only his fifth BFGoodrich Tires Trans-Am race Kenny Wilden picked the challenging Laguna Seca desert course to score his first victory. Paul Gentilozzi and Brian Simo put on their usual point trading display with Gentilozzi coming off the better of the two while notching third place. Simo ended up a lowly 29th. Boris Said drove a brand new Mustang Cobra to second place. Fourth and fifth in the finishing order went to Stu Hayner and Johnny Miller. At day's end Gentilozzi, at 247, had widened his points lead over Simo, at 218, with Jeff Altenburg registering 168 ahead of Leighton Reese, at 154, and Chris Neville, at 151. With only two events to go Simo will have to up his points production to stop Gentilozzi's bid for a third consecutive championship.

BORIS SAID HITS THE JACKPOT IN LAS VEGAS' JOHNSON CONTROLS 100

Boris Said pulled out all the stops in the Johnson Controls 100: pole position, most laps led, fastest race lap and the ultimate victory. This virtuoso performance deservedly earned him the Simple Green Clean Sweep award as well as the winner's purse. In only his second Trans-Am start, Australian Craig Baird finished second, a feat that may tempt him to contest the whole series in 2001. Third place went to Jack Willes and fourth to Willy T. Ribbs ahead of Jeff Altenburg, the final member of the top five. The placement cinched Red Line Oil Rookie of the Year honors for Altenburg. Paul Gentilozzi smacked the wall for a pointless 30th place finish. While out of the top 10, Brian Simo picked up 14 points and narrowed Gentilozzi's lead to 16 points going into the San Diego finale.

JOHNNY MILLER GETS HIS FIRST WIN IN THE SAN DIEGO SEASON FINALE

There were two big "firsts" in the San Diego finale of the 2000 BF Goodrich Tires Trans-Am campaign. Johnny Miller got his first win, holding off a strong challenge from runner-up Boris Said. Pole winner Brian Simo stayed out of trouble in his Qvale Mangusta and his conservative third place finish was good enough to earn him his first championship after two years in the runner-up role. All that 1998 and 1999 champion Paul Gentilozzi got was a broken oil pump which put him out early and put paid to his effort to record a third straight championship. He had a handsome lead with only two races to go but a pair of DNFs ended his quest. Chris Neville and Willy T. Ribbs completed the top five. For the Qvale forces it was a magnificent result, a championship in their first year.

Formula One's triumphant return to the U.S. at Indianapolis Motor Speedway was an artistic and financial smash hit. Speedway owner Tony George waved the checkered flag as Michael Schumacher won before more than a quarter million spectators, en route to championships for himself and Ferrari.

Bob Straus